RICHARD III

RICHARD III

William Shakespeare

Edited by
CEDRIC WATTS

WORDSWORTH CLASSICS

For my husband
ANTHONY JOHN RANSON
with love from your wife, the publisher.
Eternally grateful for your unconditional love.

Readers who are interested in other titles from
Wordsworth Editions are invited to visit our website at
www.wordsworth-editions.com

For our latest list and a full mail-order service, contact
Bibliophile Books, 5 Thomas Road, London E14 7BN
TEL: +44 (0)20 7515 9222 FAX: +44 (0)20 7538 4115
E-MAIL: orders@bibliophilebooks.com
WEBSITE: www.bibliophilebooks.com

This edition first published in 2015 by Wordsworth Editions Limited
8B East Street, Ware, Hertfordshire SG12 9HJ

ISBN 978 1 84022 590 7

Wordsworth Editions
is the company founded in 1987 by
MICHAEL TRAYLER

Typeset in Great Britain by Antony Gray
Printed and bound by Clays Ltd, St Ives plc

CONTENTS

GENERAL INTRODUCTION

In the Wordsworth Classics' Shakespeare Series, the inaugural volumes, *Romeo and Juliet*, *The Merchant of Venice* and *Henry V*, have been followed by *The Taming of the Shrew*, *A Midsummer Night's Dream*, *Much Ado about Nothing*, *As You Like It*, *Twelfth Night*, *Measure for Measure*, *The Winter's Tale*, *The Tempest*, *Richard II*, *Richard III*, *Henry IV Parts 1 and 2*, *Julius Cæsar*, *Hamlet*, *Othello*, *King Lear*, *Macbeth* and *Antony and Cleopatra*.

Each play in this Shakespeare Series is accompanied by a standard apparatus, including an introduction, explanatory notes and a glossary. The textual editing takes account of recent scholarship, while giving the material a careful reappraisal. The apparatus is, however, concise rather than elaborate. Every book fits a jacket pocket.

We hope that the resultant volumes prove to be handy, reliable and helpful. *The Times Literary Supplement* encouragingly states: 'Many students and ordinary readers will be grateful to Watts and his publishers for making such useful editions available at such low cost.' Furthermore, this series is now used in the workshops of the Royal Shakespeare Company.

Above all, we hope that, from Shakespeare's works, readers will derive pleasure, wisdom, provocation, challenges, and insights: insights into his culture and ours, and into the era of civilisation to which his writings have made – and continue to make – such potently influential contributions. Shakespeare's eloquence will, undoubtedly, re-echo 'in states unborn and accents yet unknown'.

CEDRIC WATTS
Series Editor

INTRODUCTION

'When I first joined the Richard III Society, someone told me he thought the play should be known as *Derek IV* – it does not depict the real Richard, so could be about anybody.'

'Now for the *Poet*, he nothing affirmeth, and therefore never lieth.'[1]

I

Shakespeare's first tetralogy of history plays, comprising the three parts of *Henry VI* plus *Richard III,* was written mainly between 1589 and 1592. In its scale, it was the greatest dramatic achievement since Aeschylus's *Oresteia*, performed in 458 BC: another tetralogy, as it consisted of three tragic dramas with a satyr-play as tailpiece. *Richard III* is lengthy, with a huge cast; and its plot is intricate, largely because it depicts the culmination of the dynastic wars enacted in the preceding plays. Accordingly, I begin with a plot-summary, my adaptation of a helpful précis by F. E. Halliday.[2] This shows that, for all the intricacies, the play is predominantly the story of one power-seeker: Richard himself.

Plot-summary:

King Edward IV is dying, and six people stand between the throne and the King's brother Richard, the ambitious, 'deformed, unfinished' Duke of Gloucester. These people are: the King's two boys, Edward (Prince of Wales) and Richard (the Duke of York), and his daughter Elizabeth; Richard's elder brother Clarence; and Clarence's young son and daughter. In the first Act, Richard succeeds in having Clarence murdered in the Tower. He then, astonishingly, by the coffin of the late Henry VI (whom he had slain), woos and wins the Lady Anne, the widow of Henry VI's son, the previous Prince of Wales, whose murderers at the Battle of Tewkesbury included Richard himself. Margaret, Henry VI's widow, plays a choric part, and warns the quarrelsome Yorkists against Richard.

When Edward IV dies, Richard, backed by Buckingham, assails the Queen's party, and executes Lord Rivers (her brother), Lord Grey (her son), and Lord Hastings (the loyal supporter of Edward's children). The young Prince Edward, now the uncrowned King Edward V, and his brother, the Duke of York, are lodged in the Tower of London ('the Princes in the Tower'). Richard has them declared illegitimate. Buckingham attempts to persuade London's citizens to proclaim Richard King. The citizens are reluctant, but hirelings of Buckingham create the illusion of popular acclaim.

As soon as Richard is crowned, he deals with his nephews and nieces: young Prince Edward and his brother are murdered in the Tower, and Richard plans to marry their sister Elizabeth after the death of his wife Anne, whose end he hastens. He will arrange for Clarence's daughter to marry a 'mean-born gentleman'. Clarence's son, being 'foolish', is not to be feared. Buckingham would not collaborate in the murder of the princes; and, being discarded by Richard, he attempts to join Richmond, but is captured and executed.

Henry Tudor, Earl of Richmond, of the House of Lancaster, returns from France, and his army confronts Richard's at Bosworth. On the night before the battle, the ghosts of those whom Richard has killed appear to him and foretell his defeat. In the battle, Richard is killed by Richmond, who is hailed as King Henry VII.

A Lancastrian claimant to the throne, Henry Tudor cemented his claim by marrying Elizabeth of York, that daughter of Edward IV and niece of Richard III. He thus ended 'the Wars of the Roses', the dynastic wars between the House of Lancaster (whose emblem was the red rose) and the House of York (whose emblem was the white rose).[3] He established the 'Tudor' dynasty, as his paternal grandfather was Owen Tudor (of Welsh origin). The Tudor rose aptly combines white and red.

Henry VII enjoyed a long reign and was succeeded by his son, Henry VIII, father of the eventual Queen Elizabeth, who was reigning when Shakespeare wrote this play.

2

Richard III was mainly written in or around 1592. From the outset, it was successful and popular: contemporaneous comments and the large number of early reprints confirm that. Richard Burbage was the star, an actor with a phenomenal range and memory. Bishop Corbet, a friend of Shakespeare's rival, Ben Jonson, described a visit to the site of the Battle of Bosworth Field: his host,

> When he would have said, '*King Richard* died,
> Calling "A horse! a horse!"' – he '*Burbage*' cried.[4]

An anecdote by John Manningham in 1602 says that a woman visiting the theatre was so impressed by Burbage's performance as Richard that she arranged to meet him that night, stipulating that he should announce himself as Richard III. Shakespeare, over-hearing this, visited her, 'was entertained and at his game ere Burbage came'.

> The message being brought that Richard III was at the door, Shakespeare caused return to be made that William the Conqueror was before Richard III.[5]

During the ensuing centuries, the play (in various manifestations, including a drastic but enduring adaptation by Colley Cibber) has remained popular, and in the last hundred years has provided a splendid vehicle for the talents of distinguished actors, among them Donald Wolfit, Laurence Olivier, Ian Holm, Antony Sher, Ian McKellen, Simon Russell Beale and Al Pacino. Those two Burbage anecdotes show that, from the outset, the play was a 'star vehicle': it was coordinated by a powerful character requiring powerful acting. Indeed, one of the themes of *Richard III* is that politics is largely play-acting: success depends on skilled per-formances. The anecdotes remind us that Richard utters famously memorable lines, notably 'A horse! A horse! My kingdom for a horse!'; and that though he says he 'cannot prove a lover', he proves to be strangely seductive. The cinema and television have magnified the play's fame. The British Film Institute claims that when the Olivier film (1955) was shown on television in the

United States of America, it gained between 25 million and 40 million viewers, outnumbering 'the sum of the play's theatrical audiences over the 358 [*sic*] years since its first performance'.[6]

As we have seen, the cast has many characters, but the action has a central clarity, because it is dominated by the figure of Richard himself: a grotesque figure, with a hunched back and withered arm, yet intensely charismatic by dint of his single-minded ruthlessness, his unflagging craftiness, and his readiness to take us – the audience – into his confidence, so that we become his (partly-unwilling, partly-willing) accomplices. His literary ancestry includes (as he tells us) 'the formal Vice, Iniquity', the wicked trickster from the Morality plays. Another ancestor is Machiavelli, who had recently made a stage appearance in the Prologue to Marlowe's *The Jew of Malta* – and that play, too, centres on an energetic, resourceful and shamelessly self-proclaimed villain. Richard had already boasted (in *Henry VI, Part 3*) that he could 'set the murderous Machiavel to school', predicting that he would kill Clarence and Edward IV's son and heir. The most Marlovian characteristic of *Richard III* is the play's dominance by a charismatic over-reacher, a man with a grudge who will seek great power and perish in the quest: Tamburlaine, Barabas, Dr Faustus and Younger Mortimer would applaud him. (Marlowe himself, a cobbler's son, mercurially successful in the theatre, a bold trouble-maker slain at the age of 29, resembles the Marlovian over-reachers.) *Richard III* also, arguably, haunts the genre of Revenge Drama, for Richard from the outset is taking revenge on a world in which nature has blighted him, so that he is

> Deformed, unfinished, sent before my time
> Into this breathing world scarce half made up,
> And that so lamely and unfashionable
> That dogs bark at me as I halt by them . . .
> And therefore, since I cannot prove a lover
> To entertain these fair well-spoken days,
> I am determinèd to prove a villain . . .

His deformity is to him a justification, a *cause* of his wicked ambition. In contrast, his enemies, who eventually become an avenging force, are inclined to see his deformity as evidence that he is essentially evil: to them the physical defects are the manifest *consequence* of innate wickedness. (Either way, Richard is undoubtedly detrimental to the cause of the physically challenged; and, being a ruthless cheat, he should be banned on sight from any paralympic games.)

The play is a good instance of ways in which, for theatregoers and readers, the aesthetic and ontological may partly or substantially subvert the ethical. (By 'aesthetic', I mean 'using a criterion of attractiveness or pleasure which disregards morality'; by the 'ontological', I mean 'using a criterion of "state of being" which, again, disregards morality'.) Of course, Richard is a wicked, callous schemer. Of course, he lies and intrigues and seeks supreme power for himself. Yet, when he is on stage, he is intense, cunning, inventive, and monstrously hypocritical: fascinating to watch: a creature from folklore and nightmare. He seems ontologically fuller (that is to say, more richly vital) than the good Richmond, who defeats him. It's a familiar literary paradox: in Jonson's *Volpone*, the wicked Volpone is amply entertaining; the virtuous Bonario is patently uninteresting. In Conrad's *Heart of Darkness*, Mr Kurtz sells his soul: but at least he had a soul to sell, unlike the 'hollow men', the unimaginative functionaries, who serve the company in Africa. In the film *The Third Man*, the corrupt Harry Lime (as played by Orson Welles) is fascinating to behold; his well-meaning, decent foe, Holly Martins, is relatively pallid. Such charismatically wicked characters solicit us to enter imaginatively a region which normally we would be too respectable, prudent and timid to enter. Admittedly, at times Richard seems deranged: he tells the lords that his arm has suddenly been withered by witchcraft, even though they know it has long been withered; and, with Buckingham, wearing grotty armour, he tries to create the illusion that an attack on the Tower may plausibly be feared, but fools nobody. Yet he still gains the crown.

Another factor complicating judgement of Richard is that he goes down fighting bravely, and he is fighting against a huge coalition: not simply the troops of Richmond, but also the forces of Heaven, for the ghosts of his victims have combined to curse him, to foretell his disaster and to urge the victory of Richmond. (Holinshed's *Chronicles* said he was visited by devils; Shakespeare deploys, instead, ghosts of victims, whose denunciations help to unify and culminate the action.) Against such a daunting confederation of the supernatural, Richard can be seen as the defiant underdog – or under-hog, according to his emblem. Morally, it's his due Nemesis: his sins have found him out: God, though slow to act, eventually acts decisively against evil. Such a reversal was predictable: Queen Margaret's curse foretold it; the Morality elements led us to expect it. Displaying more psychological inwardness and intensity than any of the other characters since Clarence, Richard undergoes a partial breakdown:

> I shall despair. There is no creature loves me;
> And if I die, no soul will pity me.
> Nay, wherefore should they, since that I myself
> Find in myself no pity to myself?

But he recovers his nerve to lead his forces defiantly into battle. Morally, his death is right; aesthetically, from the point of view of entertainment-value, his departure from the stage leaves a void.

3

One of the most striking features of *Richard III* is its formalism. A few years later, in *Henry IV, Parts 1 and 2*, Shakespeare would move strongly towards realism, offering a diversity of modes of expression, ranging from the rhetorically lofty to the colloquially vulgar. In *Richard III*, we are repeatedly aware of stylisation and even ritualisation of the speeches and action. There are passages of stichomythia (dialogue in a sequence of one-line speeches), symmetrical arrangements of speakers, parallelisms of utterance, frequent rhyming couplets, and reductive iterations of victims' names (eroding individuality, emphasising futility). Often there are long speeches to recapitulate bloody events of the past and portend a dire future; indeed, the past weighs so heavily on the present that the long era of bloodshed must, it seems, at last reach its climax and completion. In Act 1, scene 3, Queen Margaret recalls grim events and pronounces a detailed curse which will be fulfilled in the events to come. In Act 4, scene 4, Queen Margaret, Queen Elizabeth and the Duchess of York combine in a litany of woes. In Act 5, scene 4, the ghosts appear to Richard in a formalised procession, repeating to Richard, 'Despair and die', to Richmond, 'Live and flourish'. Again, the past is weighing on, and inflecting, the present. Predictably, as in Holinshed's *Chronicles*, the oration of Richmond on the eve of battle (with its recapitulation of past woes) is symmetrically matched by Richard's oration.

Shakespeare, however, was no slave of his main sources, Holinshed and Hall. He compressed, intensified and poetically enriched their accounts. He not only added those ghosts, for instance; he also lent Richard a charisma and a psychological immediacy: this intrepid schemer is outrageous yet credible. Richard also brings to mind the wicked uncle of folk-lore. In a familiar version of 'The Babes in the Wood' (the tale in ballad form), their cruel uncle commits the young boy and girl to ruffians, so that he may secure their inheritance; and although the children are not slain by the ruffians, they perish in the wood, 'in one another's arms' – bringing to mind the historic 'Princes in the Tower', betrayed by their uncle and 'Protector', portrayed embracing in the sentimental painting by Pedro Américo, and shown in death in the macabre painting by James Northcote.

Shakespeare was also aided by Seneca. There are various Senecan features in *Richard III*: for example, as in the Roman dramatist's *Thyestes*, *Phaedra* and *Octavia*, we find detailed descriptions of crimes which, as classical conventions demanded, are committed offstage; revenge is a prominent motive; curses are uttered and fulfilled; a grim underworld is described; and a vengeful ghost threatens the living. In Act 1, scene 4, of *Richard III*, Clarence's account of 'the kingdom of perpetual night', 'this dark monarchy', echoes phrasing in Seneca's *Hippolytus*, *Oedipus*, *Hercules Furens* and *Hercules Oetaeus*. Geoffrey Bullough notes that Shakespeare's introduction of three generations of women, 'each with its memories and griefs', recalls Seneca's *Troades*.[7]

The formalistic elements of *Richard III* also evoke continuity with the Greek tragic drama of the 5th Century B.C., particularly Aeschylus's *Oresteia*. In the tragic trilogy, the final play, *Eumenides*, at last brings to an end the long cycle of vengeance: the violent past is recalled, the ghost of Clytemnestra makes a plea for justice, the avenging Furies are finally placated, and a new era dawns for the city-state of Athens. *Richard III* extends but finally brings to an end the long cycle of vengeance enacted in the *Henry VI* trilogy: the violent past is recalled; the vindictive ghosts speak, strike, and are vindicated; and the new era dawns for a united England. In both cases, the internecine carnage and haunted turmoil of the past are superseded by a rational, civilised era. After a protracted painful labour and blood-flow, new birth. It is an imaginatively satisfying pattern: history is transmuted into myth.

The play's formalism is offset by passages of dark humour and descriptive richness. Some of the humorous moments stem from Richard's outrageous frankness to the audience, as when, having won Anne's consent to marriage (in Act 1, scene 2), he remarks to us:

> Was ever woman in this humour wooed?
> Was ever woman in this humour won?

In Act 1, scene 4, an incident of partly-Pinteresque humour occurs when one of the two rogues hired to murder Clarence is hesitant, suffering pangs of conscience, a temporary compassionate mood ('passionate humour'):

MURDERER 2   I hope this passionate humour of mine will change; it was wont to hold me but while one tells twenty.   [*Appropriate pause.*

MURDERER 1   How dost thou feel thyself now?

MURDERER 2   Faith, some certain dregs of conscience are yet within me.

MURDERER 1   Remember our reward, when the deed's done.

MURDERER 2   Zounds, he dies! I had forgot the reward.

Maritime scenes often called forth Shakespeare's best imaginative energies, and probably the most vivid descriptive passage in the play occurs earlier in Act 1, scene 4, when Clarence reports his nightmare, in which, drowning, he sees the strange treasures of the sea-bed:

> Inestimable stones, unvalued jewels,
> All scattered in the bottom of the sea:
> Some lay in dead men's skulls; and in the holes
> Where eyes did once inhabit, there were crept
> (As 'twere in scorn of eyes) reflecting gems,
> That wooed the slimy bottom of the deep,
> And mocked the dead bones that lay scattered by.

His descriptive account is ominous, eldritch, sensuous and

surrealistic. It pre-echoes Ariel's song in *The Tempest*: 'Full fathom five thy father lies . . . / Those are pearls that were his eyes.' It will be mocked by Clarence's eventual sordidly-grotesque drowning in the malmsey-butt. For a while, however, it deepens and makes poignant the character of Clarence, and again transmutes the political into the mythical.

4

The play purports to be depicting a historic personage, the actual King Richard III; so the following questions inevitably arise: (1) How accurate is Shakespeare's portrayal? And (2) If it is inaccurate, does that matter?

Stephen Greenblatt has stated that in the chronicle histories used by Shakespeare and in the anonymous play *The True Tragedy of Richard III*,

> Richard figures as the pitiless, treacherous villain of what has been called the 'Tudor Myth' – that is, the officially sanctioned account of the origin and legitimacy of the Tudor dynasty. That dynasty was founded by Henry, Earl of Richmond, who defeated Richard III at the Battle of Bosworth Field (1485), reigned until his death in 1509 as Henry VII, and was the grandfather of Queen Elizabeth (1533–1603). It is hardly surprising that the new regime, whose claim to the throne was somewhat shaky, would wish to discredit the old. Modern historians emphasize Richard's solid administrative skills; Tudor apologists depict Richard, the last Yorkist king, not merely as venal or unscrupulous but as a monster of evil . . . [8]

A further cautionary note is offered by the scholar John Jowett:

> Richmond's hereditary claim to the throne was weaker than Richard's. There is scope for arguing that Richard is legitimate and therefore Richmond [is] the usurper. And according to some Tudor political thinkers, whereas a usurper could be overthrown, a despotic king had to be endured.[9]

Shakespeare's main source of information about Richard was Sir Thomas More's *History of King Richard III* as incorporated in the chronicle histories by Edward Hall or Halle (1542) and by Raphael

Holinshed and others (1577, revised in 1587).[10] Thomas More, who would be declared a saint in 1935, depicted Richard as a monster:

> He was malicious, wrathful, envious, and, from before his birth, ever froward [perverse]. It is for truth reported that the Duchess, his mother, had so much ado in her travail that she could not be delivered of him uncut; and that he came into the world with the feet forward, . . . and . . . not untoothed . . . He was close and secret, a deep dissembler, lowly of countenance, arrogant of heart, outwardly compinable [companionable] where he inwardly hated, not letting [failing] to kiss whom he thought to kill, dispitious and cruel, not for evil will alway, but ofter for ambition . . . [11]

More's account was often reprinted in the 16th century: 'Government control of the press ensured that there could be no effective challenge to the "official" Tudor view of Richard III', notes John Gillingham.[12] Shakespeare, therefore, was flattering the political establishment of his day by intensifying the wickedness of Richard, giving dramatic (often melodramatic) vividness to an account that was already luridly hostile to that monarch. And Shakespeare's depiction lived on in the national memory.

Nevertheless, Richard's reputation became a matter of controversy. The biased depiction solicited the sense of 'fair play' in various readers. George Buck's *History of King Richard III* (1619) depicted Richard as valiant, wise, noble, charitable and devout, and argued that as the princes in the Tower presented no threat to Richard, he had no reason to kill them. In the following century, Horace Walpole's *Historic Doubts on the Life and Reign of King Richard the Third* (1768) alleged that the Tudor writers on Richard had asserted their biased case rather than proving it: the character of Henry VII 'was so much worse and more hateful than Richard's' (pp. 162–3), and Henry probably invented most of the slanders against Richard. In the 19th century, Sharon Turner's *The History of England during the Middle Ages* (1823) said that though Richard was guilty of the murder of his nephews, he had many good qualities: he was pious, a patron of the arts, and generally enlightened in outlook as a monarch. 'His good actions were written in water, but...his bad ones have been engraved in monumental brass' (p. 355). (Incidentally, Richard contributed generously to the construction of the magnificent chapel of King's College in Cambridge.) In the 20th century, Sir Clements Markham's *Richard III: His Life & Character Reviewed in the Light of Recent Research* (1906) claimed that Richard was innocent of the main charges against him: the real villain was Henry VII, who, according to Markham, was responsible for the murder of the princes in the Tower, probably 'between June 16 and July 16, 1486' (p. 256), and had arranged for writers to blacken the character of Richard. Markham reminds us that the history of the British monarchy has often been a story of robbery with violence.

The 'Tudor' view of Richard, however, was reinforced by two events. In 1933, the skeletons of two children, originally discovered at the Tower of London in 1674, were exhumed and given a forensic examination. The conclusion was that the bones were those of the murdered princes, Edward and his brother Richard, the Duke of York, and that they might indeed have been suffocated, as More had asserted.[13] The bones were placed in an urn in Henry VII's chapel in Westminster Abbey, together with an inscription declaring that they had been suffocated in the Tower and dishonourably buried, the blame clearly attributable to their treacherous uncle Richard, thief of the crown ('*Richardus perfidus regni praedo*').[14] 1936 saw the publication of the recently-discovered report which Dominic Mancini, a visitor from France, had submitted to the Archbishop of Vienne, an advisor to the French King. This report was presented in December 1453, the year of Richard's coronation, and recorded current rumours, particularly the rumour that Prince Edward had been killed in the Tower.

Meanwhile, in England in 1924, 'The Fellowship of the White Boar' was founded, and it was revived in the 1950s as 'The Richard III Society'. The Society was motivated by the view that a false, highly pejorative view of Richard had been propagated, and that accordingly a true account should be established. This 'Ricardian' case was reinforced by Josephine Tey's polemical novel, *The Daughter of Time* (1951). Since the 1950s, the Society (now international) has flourished. Its website in 2015 stated:

The society's view is that Shakespeare's *Richard III* is a wonderful play, with good theatre achieved through his villainous character;

however it is not history, it does not represent fact[,] and it is the
society's role to portray the real Richard III. The negative
perception of Richard III related to some or all of the following
points:

  he was a nasty hunchback who plotted and schemed his way
    to the throne;

  he killed Henry VI's son Edward;

  he killed Henry VI . . . ;

  he got his brother, the Duke of Clarence, executed;

  he killed the Princes in the Tower . . . ;

  he killed his wife Anne because he wanted to marry his niece
    Elizabeth;

  he was a bad king;

  and so it was lucky that Good King Henry Tudor got rid of
    him for us.

(As that last entry indicates, the full phrasing of the list, which I
have abbreviated, is tendentious.) Members of the Society believed
that the account of Richard's physical deformity was a derogatory
lie propagated by the pro-Tudor chroniclers. In 2013, however, a
skeleton was discovered beneath a car-park in Leicester, and
DNA tests confirmed that it was Richard's. The bones were
poignant: here were relics of the real man who had become the
mythical monster; and that man had suffered greatly, if not from
birth, probably from adolescence, and certainly in death. He had
evidently been a victim of both the cruelty of nature and the
cruelty of man. The skeleton proved that the story of Richard's
withered arm (which features prominently in the play) was
indeed a myth, for the arm-bones were sound. Nevertheless, the
skeleton displayed severe scoliosis, an S-shaped curvature of the
spine, forcing his right shoulder to be higher than his left. Thus
the most notorious physical feature of the legendary Richard, the
hump-back, became a verified fact. The curvature would have
made him shorter than the average man of the mediæval period.
It was also clear, from the severe wounds inflicted on the skull,
that Richard had died in the thick of battle, evidently on foot and
without a helmet: quite likely 'in the thickest press of his
enemies', as Polydore Vergil had claimed in his 16th-century
Anglica Historia.[15]

The gravest charge against Richard is, of course, that he, the 'Protector', was responsible for the murder of the two young princes in the Tower of London. The historian Colin Richmond has said: 'It was the belief that Richard had murdered his young (and innocent) nephew which turned many politically influential men against him' – and resulted in his eventual defeat at Bosworth.[16] In the view of the author of the continuation (1486) of the *Crowland Chronicle*, what Richard was believed to have done to his nephews in 1483 ensured his defeat in 1485: 'In this battle it was above all else the cause of those two boys, the sons of Edward IV, which was avenged.'[17] Although it cannot be proved that Richard ordered the killing of the princes, it is probable that this was the case: he had much to gain by their deaths; he was already guilty of ruthless deeds; and it was believed in his lifetime that he was responsible. One of the princes was the uncrowned King Edward V; hence, while the princes were alive, they would be a focus of rebellion. Indeed, the rebellion of October 1483 initially sought to rescue them. If they were still alive when the rumours of their deaths began to circulate, Richard could have produced them to scotch the rumours, but he did not. Guillaume de Rochefort, the French Chancellor, declared at Tours in January 1484 that Richard had killed the princes. A letter of 1 March 1486 from Mosen Diego de Valera to Ferdinand of Castile makes the same allegation. So did Jean Molinet, a Burgundian court chronicler, and so did Philippe de Commynes, a diplomat in the courts of Burgundy and France. In a chronicle by a citizen of Danzig, Caspar Weinreich, an entry for 1483 includes the statement: 'Richard the king's brother seized power and had his brother's children killed . . . ' John Gillingham concludes: 'Whatever the truth of the matter, such unanimity of international opinion is striking.'[18] When Henry VII came to power, his parliamentary Bill of Attainder against Richard declared Richard guilty of 'unnatural, mischievous, and great perjuries, treasons, homicides and murders, in shedding of infants [*sic*] blood, with many other wrongs'.[19] (Numerous recent commentators, including Charles Ross, Alison Hanham, Keith Dockray, Alison Weir, Rosemary Horrox and A. J. Pollard, have regarded Richard as the most likely suspect; though, as the Richard III Society notes, current commentaries are likely to be circumspect in phrasing.)

The allegation that Richard 'schemed his way to the throne' is readily verifiable. He arrested the unsuspecting Rivers and Grey, and later Sir Thomas Vaughan, alleging that they were conspirators and evil counsellors who would have led astray the young King Edward V. There was no durable evidence for this 'conspiracy'. The historian Colin Richmond says:

> When at Stony Stratford on the morning of 30 April [1483] he arrested Anthony Earl Rivers and Sir Richard Grey, Richard struck a deadly blow at the consensus politics the council had decided to adopt as the best form of government for the country. The council's subsequent refusal of Richard's request for the execution of Rivers and Grey was the last manifestation of such politics. To Richard that was unacceptable . . . [20]

Hence his seizure of power. Richard eliminated those members of the council who, he thought, were opposed to his plans. On 13 June, Lord Hastings, Thomas Rotherham (the Archbishop of York), John Morton (the Bishop of Ely) and Oliver King (the King's secretary) were arrested while sitting in council at the Tower. Hastings was taken out and beheaded on the spot; the others were jailed. Richard sent forth a herald to explain that a conspiracy had been discovered and the chief conspirator punished. Again, palpable evidence for the 'conspiracy' was lacking. On 16 June, many soldiers loyal to Richard (from his strongholds in the north of England) surrounded the sanctuary of Westminster Abbey to which the Queen had withdrawn with her second son, Richard of York; she was eventually persuaded to hand the son over, and he joined his brother in the Tower.

On 22 June the scheduled coronation of Edward V did not take place; on the contrary, on that day Dr Ralph Shaw preached a sermon at St Paul's Cathedral which said that Edward IV and Elizabeth Woodville had not been validly married, their children were therefore illegitimate, and Richard should accordingly take the throne. Four days later, Richard accepted the invitation. On June 25, Parliament passed the Act entitled *Titulus Regius*, declaring Richard the legitimate ruler; and on the same day, following instructions from London, the unfortunate Rivers, Grey and Vaughan were executed at Pontefract. On 6 July, Richard went to

Westminster Abbey to be crowned and anointed. Thus he had rapidly and ruthlessly gained power. Colin Richmond says that the killing of Lord Hastings was 'the moment at which Richard crossed the Rubicon': 'He revealed what one is tempted to call his heart of darkness. The message was as clear as that of Hitler on the Night of the Long Knives in June 1934.'[21]

Richard was not as *extensively* ruthless, however, as Shakespeare suggests. If Henry VI was murdered, which is probable but not certain, the most likely suspect is not Richard but Edward IV: 'no matter who carried it out, the responsibility for the deed was Edward's'.[22] Again, though Shakespeare makes Richard responsible for the death of Clarence, Clarence had in fact been prosecuted for treason by Edward IV: hence his being sentenced to death and his execution at the Tower. Even Thomas More attributes Clarence's death to King Edward, not Richard. (We may thank More for stating that Clarence was drowned in 'a Butte of Malmsey': perhaps he was; but it was certainly the bizarre kind of detail that Shakespeare liked to propagate.) In the matter of Richard's marriage to Anne: rumours circulated that Richard wished his wife to die so that he could marry his niece, Elizabeth. Richard publicly denied these rumours.[23] Anne probably died of tuberculosis (cancer remains a possibility); and, soon after her death, Richard sought to marry either Joana, sister of John II, King of Portugal, or the Infanta of Spain, and to arrange the marriage of Elizabeth of York to King John's cousin, Duke Manuel.[24] A historian, David Hammond, submits that, in any case, Richard 'was a patron of learning and the learned. He was certainly a lover of music, and an active man, courageous and exceptionally loyal to his friends'. Admittedly, 'he was also a man who showed a certain lack of principle'.[25] ('Lack of principle'? Clarence, Hastings, Rivers, Vaughan and Grey would have used more vigorous phrasing.)

Thus, Shakespeare's portrait of Richard is largely true (say, 60%), and partly false (say, 40%). Sir Philip Sidney, however, says: 'Now for the *Poet,* he nothing affirmeth, and therefore never lieth'. So a person who wished to defend Shakespeare could accordingly say, 'Shakespeare is an entertainer, a poetic playwright, not a non-fictional historian. For him, historical events are merely – and splendidly – grist to the mill of entertainment.'

Just consider the chronological liberties he takes. The death of Henry VI (whose funeral procession is depicted in Act 1, sc. 2) had taken place in 1471, but in the play is rapidly followed by the death of Edward IV, which actually happened in 1483. Stephen Greenblatt notes:

> Richard's murderous plot against his brother Clarence (1478) is cleverly twined round his cynical courtship of Lady Anne (1472), which is in turn depicted as occurring during the funeral procession of King Henry (1471).[26]

Hershel Baker adds:

> In Act I we sweep from Clarence's arrest (which occurred in 1477) and the report of Edward's final illness (1483), to a scene that conflates Henry VI's funeral (1471) and Richard's wooing of the Lady Anne, to Richard's appointment as Protector (1483), to the reappearance of old Margaret of Anjou (who had died in France in 1482), to Clarence's death by drowning in the malmsey-butt (1478).[27]

Furthermore, claims Greenblatt,

> The historical Lady Anne had only been betrothed to King Henry's son Edward, but Shakespeare writes as if she had been actually married to him; likewise, he folds Richmond's unsuccessful attempt to invade England in 1483 into his successful invasion of 1485, and he has old Queen Margaret, who was not even in England during most of the events the play depicts, haunting the royal court like a bitter, half-crazed Greek tragic chorus.[28]

John Jowett points out that Shakespeare also falsified history in order to ingratiate his company of players with men in authority.[29] Before the formation of the Lord Chamberlain's Men in 1594, it is very likely that Shakespeare worked for the company known as Lord Strange's Men, patronised by Ferdinando, Lord Strange, who was a descendant of the Lord Stanley portrayed in *Richard III*. Shakespeare veers from the main source, More's *History*, to present Stanley in a more favourable light. The play does not report the fact that Stanley helped to crush Buckingham's uprising, and it makes Lord Stanley (instead of the true leader, his brother

Sir William) the leader of the Stanley army at the Battle of Bosworth: he promises to aid Richmond during the conflict, and refuses to fight for Richard, even though Richard holds his son hostage.[30]

Again, Henry Herbert, the second Earl of Pembroke, was the patron of Lord Pembroke's Men, and there is good evidence that Shakespeare wrote for this company: the title page of the first quarto of *Titus Andronicus* (1594) says that the play was performed by three companies including Pembroke's; and the title page of the first octavo of *Henry VI, Part 3* (then called *The True Tragedie of Richard Duke of York, and the Death of Good King Henrie the Sixt*, 1595) says that it was performed by Pembroke's company. In *Richard III*, 'late in the play, [Pembroke's] ancestors Sir Walter Herbert and the Earl of Pembroke seem to be introduced solely so that they can be associated with Richmond and praised', notes Jowett; while various allusions 'strengthen the impression that Pembroke is a key figure militarily in the establishment of the Tudor monarchy, and the future king's closest confidant'.[31]

We know that Shakespeare would flatter Queen Elizabeth in *A Midsummer Night's Dream*, the Earl of Essex as well as Henry in *Henry V*, King James I (James VI of Scotland) in *Macbeth*, and King Henry VIII in *All Is True* (also known as *Henry VIII*). To that list we can add, then, that in *Richard III* he distorted history in order to flatter Ferdinando, Lord Strange, and Henry Herbert, second Earl of Pembroke; indeed, there Henry VII and the Tudor dynasty were flattered so memorably and effectively that the play would shape many people's understanding of history.

4

Richard III has been immensely successful on stage because of Shakespeare's depiction of Richard; and the play will continue to succeed, even if its distortions of history become widely recognised. We grant Shakespeare 'poetic licence'. And the real Richard was certainly ruthless, treacherous and murderous enough. Nevertheless, in the case of a different play, *Richard II*, when a historian assures us that Shakespeare's portrayal of the king is true, objectively true, this clearly enhances the play. Nigel Saul declares:

> All the most vital aspects of Richard's being . . . find a place in [Shakespeare's] reading. Shakespeare offered the insights of a dramatist and not a historian. But his characterization of the king and his understanding of what mattered to him probably bring us closer to the historical figure than many a work of history.[32]

It follows, then, that if Shakespeare in *Richard III* had been able to reconcile dramatic efficacy with a truthful and not a falsified rendering of history, the play would surely have been enhanced – wouldn't it?

One answer was given by the vivid Ian McKellen film of *Richard III* (1995), based on Richard Eyre's theatrical version.[33] This was a very free adaptation, set in a decadent England in the 1930s, when Richard establishes a fascist-style regime. As examples of the freedom of the adaptation: at a cabaret a singer (Stacey Kent) performs a swing version of Marlowe's 'The Passionate Shepherd to His Love'; and the role of Queen Margaret is subsumed within that of the Duchess of Kent. The murders are enacted with black-comic gusto. The final battle takes place in a waste-land dominated by the ruins of Battersea power-station: Richard's jeep becomes stuck in the mire, aptly prompting the King's famous cry, 'A horse! A horse! My kingdom for a horse!'.

What would Shakespeare think of such liberties? Hamlet gives the answer. When Polonius complains that a player's speech is too long, the Prince briskly responds: 'It shall to the barber's, with your beard'; and Hamlet delights in augmenting the text of *The Mousetrap*, to make it more relevant to its current audience. The full text of *Richard III* would take more than four hours on stage; in practice, it is usually cut drastically; and so it was, in Shakespeare's day, and is, in that movie. The McKellen film-adaptation of *Richard III* treats Shakespeare's text as cavalierly and imaginatively as Shakespeare treated his sources (and as those sources had treated historical reality). The film is, therefore, truer to the spirit of Shakespeare than would be a more literal, 'faithful' adaptation. And the freer the treatment, and the more we move from the earthy empirical terrain of facts to the shimmering realm of the protean and imaginary, the less important becomes the matter of historical accuracy. What then becomes conspicuous is

Shakespeare's perception of human truth: his skill as an observer of human nature and particularly of political ambition's contagion.

Yes, *Richard III* is strongly melodramatic; but so, sometimes, is history. The rise and fall of Adolf Hitler is, arguably, a modern real-life melodrama, and one which has made the monstrosity of Richard seem all too plausible. Energetically incorporating outrageous historical falsehoods, Shakespeare's *Richard III* memorably heralds appalling historical truths.

CEDRIC WATTS

NOTES TO THE INTRODUCTION

1 First quotation: Dr Lesley Boatwright, quoted on the website of the Richard III Society [U.K.]; downloaded 5.2.2015. Second quotation: Sir Philip Sidney: *The Defence of Poesie* (London: Ponsonby, 1595), p. G *recto* (no page-numbers).

2 I adapt the précis by F. E. Halliday: *A Shakespeare Companion, 1564–1964* (Harmondsworth: Penguin, 1964), p. 414. Relevant family trees are readily available on websites. Although the cast of the play seems huge, John Jowett estimates that, by means of 'doubling', all the speaking parts in the First Quarto text could be played by nine men and four boys. See John Jowett: 'Introduction' to William Shakespeare: *The Tragedy of King Richard III*, ed. John Jowett (Oxford: Oxford University Press, 2000), p. 75 footnote.

3 John Gillingham argues that Shakespeare follows Tudor chroniclers in erroneously suggesting that the Wars of the Roses caused widespread devastation. 'Indeed, . . . for the overwhelming bulk of the population, the fifteenth century...was a relatively good time in which to live.' See Gillingham's *The Wars of the Roses* (London: Weidenfeld and Nicolson, 1981), pp. 2–14; quotation, p. 11.

4 The Corbet anecdote is quoted by Jean E. Howard and Phyllis Rackin in their *Engendering a Nation: A Feminist Account of Shakespeare's English Histories* (London and New York: Routledge, 1997), p. 112. I modernise and clarify the phrasing of the couplet.

5 The Manningham anecdote is quoted by Edward Burns in *William Shakespeare: Richard III* (Horndon, Devon: Northcote House, 2006), p. 31.

6   Website: Michael Brooke: '*Richard III* (1955)': Screenonline: British Film Institute. (Downloaded 5.3.2015.) In the quotation, my '*sic*' (Latin for 'thus') means 'That's what it says (but I think it's wrong)'.

7   Geoffrey Bullough: *Narrative and Dramatic Sources of Shakespeare: Volume III: Early English History Plays*, ed. Geoffrey Bullough (London: Routledge and Kegan Paul; New York: Columbia University Press; 1960), p. 236.

8   Stephen Greenblatt: *The Norton Shakespeare*, ed. Stephen Greenblatt and others (New York and London: Norton, 1997), p. 507.

9   John Jowett: 'Introduction', p. 18.

10 Shakespeare used the second edition (London, 1587) of the *Chronicles*, Vol. 3, by Holinshed and others. The work known as Hall's *Chronicle* was originally entitled *The Union of the Two Noble and Illustrate Famelies of Lancastre and Yorke*.

11 Thomas More: *The Complete Works of St. Thomas More*, Vol. 2, ed. Richard S. Sylvester (New Haven and London: Yale University Press, 1963) pp. 7–8. See also Holinshed, p. 712. I have modernised the spelling and punctuation. The last twelve words mean 'spiteful and cruel, not always because he was evil, but more often because he was ambitious'.

12 John Gillingham: *The Wars of the Roses*, p. 10.

13 Paul M. Kendall, in *Richard the Third* (New York: Norton, 1955), p. 481, says: 'The anatomical evidence for the ages of the princes [one between 12 and 13 years, the other about 10] and for death by smothering has been held, by subsequent authorities, to be unsound...'

14 Inscription beneath the ossuary urn in Henry VII's Lady Chapel at Westminster Abbey.

15 Polydore Vergil is quoted in *Richard III: A Medieval Kingship*, ed. John Gillingham (London: Collins & Brown, 1993), p. 138. Holinshed says that Richard was slain 'manfully fighting in the middle of his enemies'. In March 2015, the ceremonial re-interment of Richard's remains at Leicester Cathedral occasioned large-scale demonstrations in which public sympathy for Richard was evident: as the cortège passed through the streets, bystanders threw white roses to deck the coffin.

16 Colin Richmond: '1483: The Year of Decision (or Taking the Throne)' in *Richard III: A Medieval Kingship*, p. 51.

17 Quoted by John Gillingham: 'Introduction: Interpreting Richard III' in *Richard III: A Medieval Kingship*, p. 14.

18 *Richard III: A Medieval Kingship*, p. 17. Pages 16–17 cite de Rochefort, de Valera, Molinet, de Commynes and Weinreich.

19 The Bill of Attainder: *Rotuli Parliamentorum*, Vol. VI, *Tempore Henrici R. VII* (London: Parliament; no date), p. 276. (I modernise the spelling and punctuation.)

20 *Richard III: A Medieval Kingship*, p. 54.

21 *Richard III: A Medieval Kingship*, p. 51.

22 John Gillingham: *The Wars of the Roses*, p. 213.

23 So says the *Crowland Chronicle*, quoted in Keith Dockray's *Richard III: A Source Book* (Stroud: Sutton, 2000), p. 99.

24 Joana (also termed Joanna) was of Lancastrian descent. See: Barry Williams: 'The Portuguese Connection and the Significance of "the Holy Princess"': *The Ricardian: Journal of the Richard III Society*, Vol. VI (March 1983), pp. 138–54; and John Ashdown-Hill: *The Last Days of Richard III* (Stroud: The History Press, 2010), pp. 26–8.

25 P. W. Hammond: 'The Reputation of Richard III' in *Richard III: A Medieval Kingship*, pp. 148–9.

26 Stephen Greenblatt: *The Norton Shakespeare*, p. 508.

27 Herschel Baker: *The Riverside Shakespeare*, ed. G. Blakemore Evans (Boston: Houghton Mifflin, 1974), p. 710.

28. Greenblatt: *The Norton Shakespeare*, p. 508. Actually, Shakespeare may be correct in saying that Anne was married to Edward; conclusive evidence of her marital or non-marital status is lacking.

29 Jowett: 'Introduction', pp. 5–6.

30 See *Richard III*, 5.3.91–6 and 5.5.3–11. In fact, Sir William Stanley sent his 3,000 men to attack Richard's forces in the rear: a crucial intervention, which resulted in Richard's defeat.

31 Jowett: 'Introduction', p. 6. See Shakespeare's *Richard III*, 4.5.12,14, and 5.3.29–32.

32 Nigel Saul: *Richard II* (New Haven, Conn.: Yale University Press, 1999), p. 466. In *Poetics* (*c.* 335 BC), Aristotle had said:
    Poetry is something more philosophical and more worthy of serious attention than history; for while poetry is concerned with universal truths, history treats of particular facts.
    See *Classical Literary Criticism*, tr. T. S. Dorsch (Harmondsworth: Penguin, 1965), pp. 43–4.

33 The film was directed by Richard Loncraine. A DVD of it has been published by Fox Pathé.

FURTHER READING
(in chronological order)

E. M. W. Tillyard: *Shakespeare's History Plays* [1944]. Harmonds-worth: Penguin, 1962.

Josephine Tey: *The Daughter of Time* [1951]. London: Arrow Books, 2009.

Narrative and Dramatic Sources of Shakespeare: Volume III: Earlier English History Plays, ed. Geoffrey Bullough. London: Routledge & Kegan Paul; New York: Columbia University Press; 1960.

John Gillingham: *The Wars of the Roses*. London: Weidenfeld and Nicolson, 1981.

Plays in Performance: 'Richard III' by William Shakespeare, ed. Juliet Hankey [1981]. Second edition: Bristol: Bristol Classical Press, 1988.

R. Chris Hassel: *Songs of Death: Performance, Interpretation, and the Text of 'Richard III'*. Lincoln, Neb., and London: University of Nebraska Press, 1987.

C. W. R. D. Moseley: *William Shakespeare: Richard III*. London: Penguin, 1989.

Hugh M. Richmond: *Shakespeare in Performance: King Richard III*. Manchester: Manchester University Press, 1989.

Barbara Hodgdon: *The End Crowns All: Closure and Contradiction in Shakespeare's History*. Princeton, N.J.: Princeton University Press, 1991.

Alison Weir: *The Princes in the Tower*. London: Bodley Head, 1992.

Richard III: A Medieval Kingship, ed. John Gillingham. London: Collins & Brown, 1993.

Jean E. Howard and Phyllis Rackin: *Engendering a Nation: A Feminist Account of Shakespeare's English Histories*. London and New York: Routledge, 1997.

John Jowett: 'Introduction' to *The Tragedy of King Richard III*, ed. John Jowett. Oxford: Oxford University Press, 2000.

Anthony Sher: *Year of the King: An Actor's Diary and Sketchbook*. London: Nick Hern Books, 2004.

Edward Burns: *William Shakespeare: 'Richard III'*. Horndon: Northcote House, 2006.

Carole M. Cusack: 'Writing about Richard III: Admissible Sources and Emotional Responses': lecture of 13 February 2010. Website of the Richard III Society of New South Wales.

Philip Schwyzer: *Shakespeare and the Remains of Richard III*. Oxford: Oxford University Press, 2013.

Cedric Watts: *Shakespeare Puzzles*. London: PublishNation, 2014.

'About Us': Website of the Richard III Society [U.K.].

NOTE ON SHAKESPEARE

William Shakespeare was the son of a glover at Stratford-upon-Avon, and tradition gives his date of birth as 23 April, 1564; certainly, three days later, he was christened at the parish church. It is likely that he attended the local Grammar School but had no university education. Of his early career there is no record, though John Aubrey reports a claim that he was a rural schoolmaster. In 1582 Shakespeare married Anne Hathaway, with whom he had two daughters, Susanna and Judith, and a son, Hamnet, who died in 1596.

How he became involved with the stage in London is uncertain, but by 1592 he was sufficiently established as a playwright to be criticised in print as a challengingly versatile 'upstart Crow'. He was a leading member of the Lord Chamberlain's company, which became the King's Men ('the King's Servants and Grooms of the Chamber') on the accession of James I in 1603. The players performed at diverse locations. Being not only a playwright and actor but also a 'sharer' (one of the owners of the company, entitled to a share of the profits), Shakespeare prospered greatly, as is proven by the numerous records of his financial transactions. Meanwhile, his sonnets depicted love for a beautiful young man and a sexual passion with a 'dark lady', and deplored the fact that, as an actor, the poet had made himself 'a motley to the view'.

Towards the end of his life, he loosened his ties with London and retired to New Place, the large house in Stratford-upon-Avon which he had bought in 1597. He died on 23 April, 1616, and is buried in the place of his baptism, Holy Trinity Church. The earliest collected edition of his plays, the First Folio, was published in 1623, and its prefatory verse-tributes include Ben Jonson's famous declaration, 'He was not of an age, but for all time'.

ACKNOWLEDGEMENTS AND TEXTUAL MATTERS

I gratefully acknowledge the help of Professor John Gillingham, the distinguished historian. Mr Antony Gray, the typesetter, was, as usual, meticulous and resourceful.

I have consulted (and am indebted to) numerous editions of *Richard III*, notably those by: Peter Alexander ('The Tudor Shakespeare': London and Glasgow: Collins, 1951; rpt., 1966); Kristian Smidt (*The Tragedy of King Richard the Third: Parallel Texts of the First Quarto and the First Folio with Variants of the Early Editions*: Oslo: Universitetsforlaget; New York: Humanities Press; 1969); G. Blakemore Evans and others ('The Riverside Shakespeare'; Boston: Houghton Mifflin, 1974); Anthony Hammond ('The Arden Shakespeare': London: Methuen, 1981); Julie Hankey ('Plays in Performance': Bristol: Bristol Classical Press, 1988); Stanley Wells and Gary Taylor (*The Complete Works: Compact Edition*: Oxford: Oxford University Press, 1988); Stephen Greenblatt and others ('The Norton Shakespeare': New York and London: Norton, 1997); Janis Lull ('The New Cambridge Shakespeare': Cambridge: Cambridge University Press, 1999); John Jowett ('The Oxford Shakespeare': Oxford: Oxford University Press, 2000); and Jonathan Bate and Eric Rasmussen ('The RSC Shakespeare', Basingstoke: Macmillan, 2008).

Next: textual matters and technical terms. A 'quarto' is a book with relatively small pages, while a 'folio' is a book with relatively large pages. A quarto volume is made of sheets of paper, each of which has been folded twice to form four leaves (and thus eight pages), whereas each of a folio's sheets has been folded once to form two leaves (and thus four pages). An 'octavo' (mentioned in the Introduction) requires three folds and yields sixteen very small pages. The 'First Folio' (often designated 'F1') was the first 'collected edition' of Shakespeare's plays, a hefty book assembled by two of the fellow-actors in his company, John Heminge (or Heminges) and Henry Condell.

The text of *Richard III* first appeared in 1597 as a quarto (Q1).

Before the F1 text was published, there appeared Q2 (1598), Q3 (1602), Q4 (1605), Q5 (1612) and Q6 (1622). Each quarto after Q1 was printed from the preceding edition, except that Q5 used both Q3 and Q4. The best texts for editorial purposes are Q1 and F1. F1 is very long; Q1 is shorter, having been cut for stage production; but Q1 contains some material absent from F1. The quarto texts of *Richard III* constituted what might be termed 'the *Richard III* material for the use of players', and the Folio text offered, so to speak, '*Richard III* for the readership of posterity'. Indeed, the Folio's editors say: 'Reade him, therefore; and againe, and againe'.

Editors who consider taking Q1 as copy-text find, accordingly, that F1 gives a fuller play and, on numerous occasions, better readings. On the other hand, editors who consider taking F1 as copy-text find that in Act 3, Shakespeare has placed Sir Richard Ratcliffe simultaneously in Yorkshire and London; and, in any case, Q1 contains some interesting material (notably the 'clock' sequence, 4.2.97-112) which is absent from F1; and Q1, in turn, can sometimes provide better readings than F1. Two sections of F1 (3.1.1-158 and from 5.3.48 to the end of Act 5) were set from a copy of Q3, and sometimes F1 adopts a reading originating in Q2-6, so in these cases Q1 is generally deemed more authentic.

Accordingly, although I have often used the fuller F1 as copy-text, on numerous occasions I have incorporated material from Q1. The endnotes give samples of the differences. Interested readers can easily consult facsimile texts of Q1 and F1, thanks to websites (e.g. that entitled 'Internet Shakespeare Editions').

The parliamentary Act of 1606 'to Restrain the Abuses of Players' forbade the utterance of holy names by actors, so that where (for instance) Q1 of *Richard III* has at one point 'Zoundes, who is there?' (i.e. 'By God's wounds, who is there?'), F1 has 'Who's there?'. In such cases, I have restored the earlier and more vigorous phrasing. In the interests of Shakespearian euphony, I have preserved such terms as 'murther', 'Divel' and 'tane', instead of modernising them as 'murder', 'Devil' and 'ta'en'. I use a dash to indicate not only an interruption to a statement, or the start of a non-consecutive statement, but also a change of direction when a speaker turns from one addressee to another. To preserve the pentameter (five usually-iambic metrical feet per line), I have marked with an acute accent a normally-unstressed or apparently-unstressed syllable which needs to be stressed (e.g. 'And in recórd'), and with a grave accent a normally-unsounded vowel which needs to be sounded (e.g. 'perturbatiòns').

The present edition thus offers a practical compromise between: (a) those early texts; (b) Shakespeare's intentions, insofar as they can be reasonably inferred; and (c) modern requirements. My general aim is to attain maximum clarification with minimum alteration, while respecting the stylistic qualities of the verse.

The glossary explains archaisms and unfamiliar terms. The annotations offer clarification of obscurities, while drawing attention to textual variations. I have endeavoured to be concise, hoping that the resultant book will slip easily into a pocket, bag or wallet-file.

No edition of this play can claim to be definitive. This edition aspires to be *useful*.

THE TRAGEDY OF
KING RICHARD THE THIRD

CHARACTERS:

KING EDWARD IV.

His mother: THE DUCHESS OF YORK.

His sons: PRINCE EDWARD *(later, his Ghost)*
and RICHARD, *the young* DUKE OF YORK *(later, his Ghost).*

His brothers: GEORGE, DUKE OF CLARENCE *(later, his Ghost),*
and RICHARD, DUKE OF GLOUCESTER, *later King Richard III.*

CLARENCE'S SON *and* DAUGHTER *(Edwin and Margaret
  Plantagenet).*

Wife of King Edward IV: QUEEN ELIZABETH.

Her brother: ANTHONY WOODVILLE, EARL RIVERS *(later, his
  Ghost).*

Her sons: THE MARQUIS OF DORSET
and LORD GREY *(later, his Ghost).*

SIR THOMAS VAUGHAN *(later, his Ghost).*

SIR WILLIAM BRANDON.

THOMAS HOWARD, THE EARL OF SURREY.

LORD LOVEL.

KING HENRY VI *(deceased; later, his Ghost).*

QUEEN MARGARET, *widow of King Henry VI.*

GHOST *of* PRINCE EDWARD, *son of King Henry VI.*

LADY ANNE, *widow of Prince Edward (later, her Ghost).*

Lady Anne's attendants: TRESSEL *and* BERKELEY.

WILLIAM, LORD HASTINGS, *the Lord Chamberlain (later, his
  Ghost).*

LORD STANLEY, THE EARL OF DEBY, *friend of Hastings.*

HENRY, THE EARL OF RICHMOND, *Stanley's son-in-law, later
  King Henry VII.*

Richmond's followers:
THE EARL OF OXFORD,
SIR JAMES BLUNT
and SIR WALTER HERBERT.

Followers of Richard, Duke of Gloucester:
THE DUKE OF BUCKINGHAM *(later, his Ghost),*
THE DUKE OF NORFOLK,
THE EARL OF SURREY, *Norfolk's son,*
SIR RICHARD RATCLIFFE,
SIR WILLIAM CATESBY,
SIR JAMES TYRREL,
TWO MURDERERS
and a PAGE.

Ecclesiastics:
LORD CARDINAL BOURCHIER, *Archbishop of Canterbury,*
THE ARCHBISHOP OF YORK,
THE BISHOP OF ELY,
TWO OTHER BISHOPS,
SIR JOHN, *a priest,*
and SIR CHRISTOPHER URSWICK, *another priest.*

SIR ROBERT BRAKENBURY, *Lieutenant and Keeper of the Tower of London.*
THE LORD MAYOR *of London.*
A SCRIVENER.
A PURSUIVANT.
A SHERIFF.
LORDS, NOBLEMEN, ALDERMEN, GENTLEMEN, CITIZENS, SOLDIERS, HALBERDIERS, DRUMMERS, TRUMPETERS, MESSENGERS, ATTENDANTS, *etc.*

THE TRAGEDY OF KING RICHARD THE THIRD[1]

ACT I, SCENE I.

London. A street.

Enter RICHARD, *Duke of Gloucester.*

RICHARD Now is the winter of our discontent
Made glorious summer by this sun of York;[2]
And all the clouds that loured upon our House
In the deep bosom of the ocean buried.
Now are our brows bound with victorious wreaths,
Our bruisèd arms hung up for monuments,
Our stern alarums changed to merry meetings,
Our dreadful marches to delightful measures.
Grim-visaged War hath smoothed his wrinkled front;
And now, instead of mounting barbèd steeds 10
To fright the souls of fearful advers'ries,
He capers nimbly in a lady's chamber,
To the lascivious pleasing of a lute.
But I, that am not shaped for sportive tricks,
Nor made to court an amorous looking-glass;
I, that am rudely stamped, and want love's majesty
To strut before a wanton ambling nymph;
I, that am curtailed of this fair proportion,
Cheated of feature by dissembling Nature,
Deformed, unfinished, sent before my time 20
Into this breathing world scarce half made up,
And that so lamely and unfashionable
That dogs bark at me as I halt by them;
Why, I, in this weak piping-time of peace,
Have no delight to pass away the time,
Unless to spy my shadow in the sun
And descant on mine own deformity.
And therefore, since I cannot prove a lover
To entertain these fair well-spoken days,
I am determinèd to prove a villain, 30
And hate the idle pleasures of these days.
Plots have I laid, inductions dangerous,

By drunken prophecies, libels and dreams,
To set my brother Clarence and the King
In deadly hate, the one against the other;
And if King Edward be as true and just
As I am subtle, false and treacherous,
This day should Clarence closely be mewed up,
About a prophecy, which says that 'G'
Of Edward's heirs the murderer shall be.[3]   40
– Dive, thoughts, down to my soul: here Clarence
                                                      comes.

Enter George, Duke of CLARENCE, *between* GUARDS, *with Sir Robert*
        BRAKENBURY, *Lieutenant of the Tower.*

        – Brother, good day. What means this armèd guard
That waits upon your Grace?
CLARENCE   His Majesty,
Tend'ring my person's safety, hath appointed
This conduct to convey me to the Tower.
RICHARD   Upon what cause?
CLARENCE   Because my name is George.
RICHARD   Alack, my Lord, that fault is none of yours:
He should, for that, commit your godfathers.[4]
O, belike his Majesty hath some intent
That you should be new-christened in the Tower.   50
But what's the matter, Clarence: may I know?
CLARENCE Yea, Richard, when I know; but I protest,
As yet I do not. But, as I can learn,
He hearkens after prophecies and dreams,
And from the cross-row plucks the letter G,
And says a wizard told him that by 'G'
His issue disinherited should be;
And for my name of George begins with G,
It follows in his thought that I am he.
These (as I learn) and such-like toys as these   60
Hath moved his Highness to commit me now.
RICHARD   Why, this it is, when men are ruled by women:
'Tis not the King that sends you to the Tower;
My Lady Grey his wife, Clarence, 'tis she
That tempers him to this extremity.[5]
Was it not she, and that good man of worship,

Anthony Woodvílle, her brother there,[6]
That made him send Lord Hastings to the Tower,
From whence this present day he is delivered?
We are not safe, Clarence, we are not safe!   70

CLARENCE By Heaven, I think there is no man secure
But the Queen's kindred, and night-walking heralds
That trudge betwixt the King and Mistress Shore.[7]
Heard you not what an humble suppliant
Lord Hastings was to her for his delivery?

RICHARD Humbly complaining to her deity
Got my Lord Chamberlain his liberty.
I'll tell you what: I think it is our way,
If we will keep in favour with the King,
To be her men and wear her livery.   80
The jealous o'er-worn widow[8] and herself,
Since that our brother dubbed them gentlewomen,
Are mighty gossips in our monarchy.

BRAKEN. I beseech your Graces both to pardon me:
His Majesty hath straitly given in charge
That no man shall have private conference
(Of what degree soever) with his brother.

RICHARD Even so; an't please your Worship, Brakenbury,
You may partake of anything we say:
We speak no treason, man: we say the King   90
Is wise and virtuous, and his noble Queen
Well struck in years, fair, and not jealous;
We say that Shore's wife hath a pretty foot,
A cherry lip, a bonny eye, a passing pleasing tongue;
And that the Queen's kin are made gentlefolks.
How say you, sir? Can you deny all this?

BRAKEN. With this, my Lord, myself have nought to do.

RICHARD Naught to do with Mistress Shore? I tell thee, fellow,
He that doth naught with her (excepting one)
Were best to do it secretly, alone.   100

BRAKEN. What one, my Lord?

RICHARD Her husband, knave: wouldst thou betray me?

BRAKEN. I do beseech your Grace to pardon me, and withal
Forbear your conference with the noble Duke.

CLARENCE We know thy charge, Brakenbury, and will obey.

RICHARD   We are the Queen's abjects, and must obey.
           Brother, farewell: I will unto the King,
           And whatsoe'er you will employ me in,
           Were it to call King Edward's widow 'sister',
           I will perform it to enfranchise you.   110
           Meantime, this deep disgrace in brotherhood
           Touches me dearer than you can imagine.
                         [*He embraces Clarence, weeping.*[9]

CLARENCE   I know it pleaseth neither of us well.

RICHARD   Well, your imprisonment shall not be long:
           I will deliver you, or else lie for you;[10]
           Meantime, have patience.

CLARENCE   I must perforce. Farewell.
               [*Exeunt Clarence, Brakenbury and the guards.*

RICHARD   Go, tread the path that thou shalt ne'er return.
           Simple, plain Clarence, I do love thee so,
           That I will shortly send thy soul to Heaven,
           If Heaven will take the present at our hands.   120
           – But who comes here? The new-delivered Hastings?

Enter Lord HASTINGS.

HASTINGS   Good time of day unto my gracious Lord!

RICHARD   As much unto my good Lord Chamberlain!
           Well are you welcome to the open air.
           How hath your Lordship brooked imprisonment?

HASTINGS   With patience, noble Lord, as prisoners must;
           But I shall live, my Lord, to give them thanks
           That were the cause of my imprisonment.

RICHARD   No doubt, no doubt; and so shall Clarence too,
           For they that were your enemies are his,   130
           And have prevailed as much on him as you.

HASTINGS   More pity that the eagles should be mewed,
           While kites and buzzards prey at liberty.

RICHARD   What news abroad?

HASTINGS   No news so bad abroad as this at home:
           The King is sickly, weak, and melancholy,
           And his physicians fear him mightily.

RICHARD   Now, by Saint John, that news is bad indeed!
           O, he hath kept an evil diet long,
           And overmuch consumed his royal person: 140

'Tis very grievous to be thought upon.
Where is he, in his bed?

HASTINGS   He is.

RICHARD   Go you before, and I will follow you.   [*Exit Hastings.*
He cannot live, I hope; and must not die
Till George be packed with post-horse up to Heaven.
I'll in, to urge his hatred more to Clarence
With lies well-steeled with weighty arguments;
And, if I fail not in my deep intent,
Clarence hath not another day to live;
Which done, God take King Edward to His mercy,   150
And leave the world for me to bustle in!
For then I'll marry Warwick's youngest daughter.
What though I killed her husband and her father?[11]
The readiest way to make the wench amends
Is to become her husband and her father:[12]
The which will I; not all so much for love
As for another secret close intent,
By marrying her, which I must reach unto.
But yet I run before my horse to market:
Clarence still breathes, Edward still lives and reigns;   160
When they are gone, then must I count my gains.
                                         [*Exit.*

SCENE 2.

London. A street.

Enter GENTLEMEN *(accompanied by* HALBERDIERS*) bearing the open
coffin of* KING HENRY VI, *followed by Lady* ANNE *in mourning,*
TRESSEL *and* BERKELEY.

ANNE   Set down, set down your honourable load
(If honour may be shrouded in a hearse),
Whilst I awhile obsequiously lament
Th'untimely fall of virtuous Lancaster.
                         [*They set the coffin down.*
Poor key-cold figure of a holy king,
Pale ashes of the House of Lancaster,

Thou bloodless remnant of that royal blood:
Be it lawful that I invocate thy ghost
To hear the lamentations of poor Anne,
Wife to thy Edward, to thy slaughtered son,   10
Stabbed by the selfsame hand that made these wounds.
Lo, in these windows that let forth thy life
I pour the helpless balm of my poor eyes.
O cursèd be the hand that made these holes!
Cursèd the heart that had the heart to do it!
Cursèd the blood that let this blood from hence!
More direful hap betide that hated wretch
That makes us wretched by the death of thee
Than I can wish to adders,[13] spiders, toads,
Or any creeping venomed thing that lives!   20
If ever he have child, abortive be it,
Prodigious, and untimely brought to light,
Whose ugly and unnatural aspéct
May fright the hopeful mother at the view,
And that be heir to his unhappiness!
If ever he have wife, let her be made
More miserable by the death of him
Than I am made by my young Lord and thee![14]
– Come, now towards Chertsey with your holy load,
Taken from Paul's to be interrèd there;[15]   30
                       [*The gentlemen lift the coffin.*
And still, as you are weary of this weight,
Rest you, whiles I lament King Henry's corse.

                 Enter RICHARD.

RICHARD   Stay, you that bear the corse, and set it down!
ANNE   What black magician conjures up this fiend,
             To stop devoted charitable deeds?
RICHARD   Villains, set down the corse; or, by Saint Paul,
             I'll make a corse of him that disobeys!
HALBERD.   My Lord, stand back, and let the coffin pass.
RICHARD   Unmannered dog, stand thou, when I command!
             Advance thy halberd higher than my breast,   40
             Or, by Saint Paul, I'll strike thee to my foot,
             And spurn upon thee, beggar, for thy boldness.
                       [*They set the coffin down.*

ANNE   – What, do you tremble? Are you all afraid?
             Alas, I blame you not, for you are mortal,
             And mortal eyes cannot endure the Divel.[16]
             – Avaunt, thou dreadful minister of Hell!
             Thou hadst but power over his mortal body;
             His soul thou canst not have: therefore, be gone.

RICHARD   Sweet saint, for charity, be not so curst.

ANNE   Foul Divel, for God's sake hence and trouble us not,   50
             For thou hast made the happy earth thy Hell,
             Filled it with cursing cries and deep exclaims.
             If thou delight to view thy heinous deeds,
             Behold this pattern of thy butcheries.
             – O, gentlemen, see, see! Dead Henry's wounds
             Open their cóngealed mouths and bleed afresh.[17]
             – Blush, blush, thou lump of foul deformity,
             For 'tis thy presence that exhales this blood
             From cold and empty veins where no blood dwells;
             Thy deeds, inhuman and unnatural,   60
             Provokes this deluge most unnatural.
             – O God, Which this blood mad'st, revenge his death!
             – O earth, which this blood drink'st, revenge his death!
             Either Heaven with lightning strike the murth'rer dead,
             Or earth gape open wide and eat him quick,
             As thou dost swallow up this good King's blood,
             Which his Hell-governed arm hath butcherèd!

RICHARD   Lady, you know no rules of charity,
             Which renders good for bad, blessings for curses.

ANNE   Villain, thou know'st no law of God nor man: 70
             No beast so fierce but knows some touch of pity.

RICHARD   But I know none, and therefore am no beast.

ANNE   O wonderful, when divels tell the truth![18]

RICHARD   More wonderful, when angels are so angry.
             Vouchsafe (divine perfection of a woman),
             Of these supposèd crimes to give me leave,
             By circumstance, but to acquit myself.

ANNE   Vouchsafe (diffused infection of a man),
             Of these known evils but to give me leave,
             By circumstance, to accuse[19] thy cursèd self.   80

RICHARD   Fairer than tongue can name thee, let me have

	Some patient leisure to excuse myself.
ANNE	Fouler than heart can think thee, thou canst make
	No excuse current but to hang thyself.
RICHARD	By such despair, I should accuse myself.
ANNE	And by despairing shalt thou stand excused
	For doing worthy vengeance on thyself
	That didst unworthy slaughter upon others.
RICHARD	Say that I slew them not?
ANNE	Then say they were not slain:[20]
	But dead they are, and, divelish slave, by thee. 90
RICHARD	I did not kill your husband.
ANNE	Why, then he is alive.
RICHARD	Nay, he is dead; and slain by Edward's hands.
ANNE	In thy foul throat thou liest: Queen Margaret saw
	Thy murd'rous falchion smoking in his blood,
	The which thou once didst bend against her breast,
	But that thy brothers beat aside the point.[21]
RICHARD	I was provokèd by her sland'rous tongue,
	That laid their guilt upon my guiltless shoulders.
ANNE	Thou wast provokèd by thy bloody mind,
	That never dream'st on aught but butcheries. 100
	Didst thou not kill this King?
RICHARD	I grant ye, yea.[22]
ANNE	Dost 'grant' me, hedgehog? Then God grant me too
	Thou mayst be damnèd for that wicked deed!
	O he was gentle, mild, and virtuous.
RICHARD	The better for the King of Heaven that hath him.
ANNE	He is in Heaven, where thou shalt never come.
RICHARD	Let him thank me, that holp to send him thither;
	For he was fitter for that place than earth.
ANNE	And thou unfit for any place but Hell.
RICHARD	Yes, one place else, if you will hear me name it. 110
ANNE	Some dungeon.
RICHARD	Your bed-chamber.
ANNE	Ill rest betide the chamber where thou liest!
RICHARD	So will it, madam, till I lie with you.
ANNE	I hope so.
RICHARD	I know so. But, gentle Lady Anne,
	To leave this keen encounter of our wits,

	And fall something into a slower method:	
	Is not the causer of the timeless deaths
	Of these Plantagenets, Henry and Edward,
	As blameful as the executioner?
ANNE	Thou wast the cause and most accursed effect.[23]	120
RICHARD	Your beauty was the cause of that effect:
	Your beauty, that did haunt me in my sleep
	To undertake the death of all the world,
	So I might live one hour in your sweet bosom.
ANNE	If I thought that, I tell thee, homicide,
	These nails should rend that beauty from my cheeks.
RICHARD	These eyes could not endure that beauty's wrack;
	You should not blemish it, if I stood by:
	As all the world is cheered by the sun,
	So I by that: it is my day, my life.	130
ANNE	Black night o'ershade thy day, and death thy life!
RICHARD	Curse not thyself, fair creature; thou art both.
ANNE	I would I were, to be revenged on thee.[24]
RICHARD	It is a quarrel most unnatural,
	To be revenged on him that loveth thee.
ANNE	It is a quarrel just and reasonable,
	To be revenged on him that killed my husband.
RICHARD	He that bereft thee, lady, of thy husband,
	Did it to help thee to a better husband.
ANNE	His better doth not breathe upon the earth.	140
RICHARD	He lives that loves thee better than he could.
ANNE	Name him.
RICHARD	Plantagenet.
ANNE	Why, that was he,[25]
RICHARD	The selfsame name, but one of better nature.
ANNE	Where is he?
RICHARD	Here. [*She spits at him.*
	Why dost thou spit at me?
ANNE	Would it were mortal poison, for thy sake!
RICHARD	Never came poison from so sweet a place.
ANNE	Never hung poison on a fouler toad.[26]
	Out of my sight! Thou dost infect mine eyes.
RICHARD	Thine eyes, sweet lady, have infected mine.
ANNE	Would they were basilisks, to strike thee dead!	150

RICHARD   I would they were, that I might die at once;
                For now they kill me with a living death.
                Those eyes of thine from mine have drawn salt tears,
                Shamed their aspécts with store of childish drops:
                These eyes, which never shed remorseful tear,
                No, when my father York and Edward wept
                To hear the piteous moan that Rutland made
                When black-faced Clifford shook his sword at him;
                Nor when thy warlike father, like a child,
                Told the sad story of my father's death,[27]   160
                And twenty times made pause to sob and weep,
                That all the standers-by had wet their cheeks
                Like trees bedashed with rain. In that sad time,
                My manly eyes did scorn an humble tear;
                And what these sorrows could not thence exhale,
                Thy beauty hath, and made them blind with weeping.[28]
                I never sued to friend nor enemy;
                My tongue could never learn sweet smoothing word;
                But, now thy beauty is proposed my fee,
                My proud heart sues, and prompts my tongue to speak. 170
                              [She looks scornfully at him.
                Teach not thy lip such scorn, for it was made
                For kissing, lady, not for such contempt.
                If thy revengeful heart cannot forgive,
                       [He kneels and offers her his sword.
                Lo, here I lend thee this sharp-pointed sword;
                Which if thou please to hide in this true breast,
                And let the soul forth that adoreth thee,
                I lay it naked to the deadly stroke,
                And humbly beg the death upon my knee.
             [He bares his breast; she aims the sword at it, but pauses.
                Nay, do not pause, for I did kill King Henry;
                But 'twas thy beauty that provokèd me.   180
                Nay, now dispatch: 'twas I that stabbed young Edward;
                But 'twas thy heavenly face that set me on.
                                  [She drops the sword.
                Take up the sword again, or take up *me.*

ANNE   Arise, dissembler: though I wish thy death,
                I will not be thy executioner.

[He rises.

RICHARD	Then bid me kill myself, and I will do it.
ANNE	I have already.
RICHARD	That was in thy rage:

Speak it again, and, even with the word,
This hand, which, for thy love, did kill thy love,
Shall, for thy love, kill a far truer love: 190
To both their deaths shalt thou be accessory.

ANNE	I would I knew thy heart.
RICHARD	'Tis figured in my tongue.
ANNE	I fear me, both are false.
RICHARD	Then never was man true.
ANNE	Well, well, put up your sword.
RICHARD	Say, then, my peace is made.
ANNE	That shalt thou know hereafter.
RICHARD	But shall I live in hope?
ANNE	All men, I hope, live so. 200
RICHARD	Vouchsafe to wear this ring.
ANNE	To take is not to give. *[He puts the ring on her finger.*
RICHARD	Look how my ring encompasseth thy finger:

Even so thy breast encloseth my poor heart;
Wear both of them, for both of them are thine.
And if thy poor devoted servant may
But beg one favour at thy gracious hand,
Thou dost confirm his happiness for ever.

ANNE	What is it?
RICHARD	That it may please you leave these sad designs 210

To him that hath most cause to be a mourner,
And presently repair to Crosby House;[29]
Where (after I have solemnly interred
At Chertsey monast'ry this noble King,
And wet his grave with my repentant tears)
I will with all expedient duty see you.
For divers unknown reasons, I beseech you,
Grant me this boon.

ANNE	With all my heart; and much it joys me, too,

To see you are become so penitent.   220
– Tressel and Berkeley, go along with me.

RICHARD	Bid me farewell.

ANNE   'Tis more than you deserve;
          But since you teach me how to flatter you,
          Imagine I have said 'farewell' already.
                              [*Exeunt Tressel and Berkeley with Anne.*
RICHARD   Sirs, take up the corse.
HALBERDIER   Towards Chertsey, noble Lord?
RICHARD   No, to Whitefriars;[30] there attend my coming.
                    [*Exeunt gentlemen and halberdiers with the coffin.*
          Was ever woman in this humour wooed?
          Was ever woman in this humour won?
          I'll have her; but I will not keep her long.
          What? I, that killed her husband and his father,   230
          To take her in her heart's extremest hate,
          With curses in her mouth, tears in her eyes,
          The bleeding witness of my hatred by;
          Having God, her conscience, and these bars against me,
          And I no friends to back my suit at all,
          But the plain Divel and dissembling looks,
          And yet to win her! All the world to nothing![31]
          Ha!
          Hath she forgot already that brave Prince,
          Edward, her Lord, whom I, some three months since,   240
          Stabbed in my angry mood at Tewkesbury?
          A sweeter and a lovelier gentleman,
          Framed in the prodigality of Nature,[32]
          Young, valiant, wise, and (no doubt) right royal,
          The spacious world cannot again afford:
          And will she yet abase her eyes on me,
          That cropped the golden prime of this sweet Prince,
          And made her widow to a woeful bed?
          On me, whose all not equals Edward's moiety?
          On me, that halts and am misshapen thus?   250
          My Dukedom to a beggarly denier,
          I do mistake my person all this while:
          Upon my life, she finds (although I cannot)
          Myself to be a marv'llous proper man.
          I'll be at charges for a looking-glass,
          And entertain a score or two of tailors
          To study fashions to adorn my body:

Since I am crept in favour with myself,
I will maintain it with some little cost.
But first I'll turn yon fellow in his grave,   260
And then return lamenting to my love.
Shine out, fair sun, till I have bought a glass,
That I may see my shadow as I pass.   [*Exit.*

SCENE 3.

London. The Palace.

Enter QUEEN ELIZABETH, *Lord* RIVERS, *Lord* GREY
and the Marquis of DORSET.

RIVERS   Have patience, madam: there's no doubt his Majesty
            Will soon recover his accustomed health.

GREY   In that you brook it ill, it makes him worse;
            Therefore, for God's sake, entertain good comfort,
            And cheer his Grace with quick and merry eyes.

Q. ELIZAB. If he were dead, what would betide on me?

GREY   No other harm but loss of such a lord.

Q. ELIZAB. The loss of such a lord includes all harms.

GREY   The Heavens have blessed you with a goodly son,
            To be your comforter when he is gone.   10

Q. ELIZAB. Ah, he is young, and his minority
            Is put unto the trust of Richard Gloucester,
            A man that loves not me, nor none of you.

RIVERS   Is it concluded he shall be Protector?

Q. ELIZAB. It is determined, not concluded yet;
            But so it must be, if the King miscarry.

Enter the Duke of BUCKINGHAM *with* STANLEY, *Earl of Derby.*

GREY   Here come the Lords of Buckingham and Derby.

BUCKING. [*to Eliz.:*] Good time of day unto your royal Grace!

STANLEY [*to Eliz.:*] God make your Majesty joyful,
                                as you have been!

Q. ELIZAB. The Countess Richmond, good my Lord of Derby,   20
            To your good prayer will scarcely say 'Amen'.
            Yet, Derby, notwithstanding she's your wife,
            And loves not me, be you, good Lord, assured
            I hate not you for her proud arrogance.[33]

STANLEY	I do beseech you, either not believe
	The envious slanders of her false accusers,
	Or, if she be accused on true report,
	Bear with her weakness, which I think proceeds
	From wayward sickness, and no grounded malice.
Q. ELIZAB.	Saw you the King today, my Lord of Derby? 30
STANLEY	But now the Duke of Buckingham and I
	Are come from visiting his Majesty.
Q. ELIZAB.	What likelihood of his amendment, Lords?
BUCKING.	Madam, good hope; his Grace speaks cheerfully.
Q. ELIZAB.	God grant him health! Did you confer with him?
BUCKING.	Ay, madam: he desires to make atonement
	Between the Duke of Gloucester and your brothers,
	And between them and my Lord Chamberlain;³⁴
	And sent to warn them to his royal presence.
Q. ELIZAB.	Would all were well! But that will never be; 40
	I fear our happiness is at the height.³⁵

Enter RICHARD *and* HASTINGS.

RICHARD	They do me wrong, and I will not endure it!
	Who is it that complains unto the King,
	That I (forsooth) am stern and love them not?
	By holy Paul, they love his Grace but lightly
	That fill his ears with such dissentious rumours.
	Because I cannot flatter and look fair,
	Smile in men's faces, smooth, deceive and cog,
	Duck with French nods and apish courtesy,
	I must be held a rancorous enemy. 50
	Cannot a plain man live and think no harm,
	But thus his simple truth must be abused
	With silken, sly, insinuating Jacks?
GREY	To whom in all this presence speaks your Grace?
RICHARD	To thee, that hast nor honesty nor grace.
	When have I injured thee? When done thee wrong?
	– Or thee? – Or thee? – Or any of your faction?
	A plague upon you all! His royal Grace
	(Whom God preserve better than you would wish!)
	Cannot be quiet scarce a breathing while, 60
	But you must trouble him with lewd complaints.
Q. ELIZAB.	Brother of Gloucester, you mistake the matter.

The King, on his own royal disposition,
And not provoked by any suitor else,
Aiming (belike) at your interior hatred,
That in your outward action shows itself
Against my children, brothers, and myself,
Makes him to send, that he may learn the ground
Of your ill-will, and thereby to remove it.[36]

RICHARD   I cannot tell; the world is grown so bad
That wrens make prey where eagles dare not perch.   70
Since every Jack became a gentleman,
There's many a gentle person made a Jack.

Q. ELIZAB.   Come, come, we know your meaning, brother
                                                    Gloucester:
You envy my advancement and my friends'.
God grant we never may have need of you!

RICHARD   Meantime, God grants that I have need of *you*.
Our brother[37] is imprisoned by your means,
Myself disgraced, and the nobility
Held in contempt, while great promotiòns
Are daily given to ennoble those   80
That scarce some two days since were worth a noble.

Q. ELIZAB.   By Him that raised me to this careful height
From that contented hap which I enjoyed,
I never did incense his Majesty
Against the Duke of Clarence, but have been
An earnest advocate to plead for him.
My Lord, you do me shameful injury,
Falsely to draw me in these vile suspécts.

RICHARD   You may deny that you were not the mean
Of my Lord Hastings' late imprisonment.   90

RIVERS   She may, my Lord, for –

RICHARD   'She may', Lord Rivers? Why, who knows not so?
She may do more, sir, than denying that:
She may help you to many fair preferments
And then deny her aiding hand therein,
And lay those honours on your high desert.
What may she not? She may – ay, marry, may she –

RIVERS   What 'marry, may she'?

RICHARD   What, *marry* may she! Marry with a king,[38]

	A bachelor, and a handsome stripling too:	100
	Iwis your grandam had a worser match.	
Q. ELIZAB.	My Lord of Gloucester, I have too long borne	
	Your blunt upbraidings and your bitter scoffs:	
	By Heaven, I will acquaint his Majesty	
	Of those gross taunts that oft I have endured.	
	I had rather be a country servant-maid	
	Than a great queen with this conditiòn,	
	To be so baited, scorned, and stormèd at.	

Enter old QUEEN MARGARET, *unseen, behind them.*

	Small joy have I in being England's Queen.	
Q. MARG.	[*aside:*] And lessened be that small, God I beseech Him!	110
	Thy honour, state, and seat is due to me.	
RICHARD	[*to Eliz.:*] What! Threat you me with telling of the King?	
	Tell him, and spare not: look what I have said,[39]	
	I will avouch't in presence of the King:	
	I dare adventure to be sent to th'Tower.	
	'Tis time to speak; my pains are quite forgot.	
Q. MARG.	[*aside:*] Out, divel! I do remember them too well:	
	Thou kill'dst my husband Henry in the Tower,	
	And Edward, my poor son, at Tewkesbury.	
RICHARD	[*to Eliz.:*] Ere you were Queen, ay, or your husband King,	120
	I was a pack-horse in his great affairs:	
	A weeder-out of his proud advers'ries,	
	A liberal rewarder of his friends:	
	To royalise his blood, I spent mine own.	
Q. MARG.	[*aside:*] Ay, and much better blood than his or thine.	
RICHARD	[*to Eliz.:*] In all which time you and your husband Grey	
	Were factious for the House of Lancaster;	
	– And, Rivers, so were you. – Was not your husband	
	In Margaret's battle at Saint Albans slain?	
	Let me put in your minds, if you forget,	130
	What you have been ere this, and what you are;	
	Withal, what I have been, and what I am.	
Q. MARG.	[*aside:*] A murth'rous villain, and so still thou art.	
RICHARD	Poor Clarence did forsake his father, Warwick;	
	Ay, and forswore himself – which Jesu pardon! – [40]	
Q. MARG.	[*aside:*] Which God revenge!	
RICHARD	To fight on Edward's party for the crown;	

And for his meed, poor Lord, he is mewed up.
I would to God my heart were flint, like Edward's,
Or Edward's soft and pitiful, like mine: 140
I am too childish-foolish for this world.

Q. MARG.   [*aside:*] Hie thee to Hell for shame, and leave this world,
Thou cacodemon! There thy kingdom is.

RIVERS   My Lord of Gloucester: in those busy days
Which here you urge to prove us enemies,
We followed then our Lord, our sovereign King:
So should we you, if you should be our King.

RICHARD   If I should be? I had rather be a pedlar:
Far be it from my heart, the thought thereof.

Q. ELIZAB. As little joy, my Lord, as you suppose   150
You should enjoy, were you this country's King,
As little joy you may suppose in me
That I enjoy, being the Queen thereof.

Q. MARG.   [*aside:*] As little joy enjoys the Queen thereof;
For I am she, and altogether joyless.
I can no longer hold me patiènt.

She comes forward and addresses them.

Hear me, you wrangling pirates, that fall out
In sharing that which you have pilled from me:
Which of you trembles not that looks on me?
If not, that I am Queen, you bow like subjects,   160
Yet that, by you deposed, you quake like rebels.[41]
[*To Richard:*] Ah, gentle villain, do not turn away!

RICHARD   Foul wrinkled witch, what mak'st thou in my sight?

Q. MARG.   But repetition of what thou hast marred;
That will I make before I let thee go.

RICHARD   Wert thou not banishèd on pain of death?

Q. MARG.   I was; but I do find more pain in banishment
Than death can yield me here by my abode.[42]
A husband and a son thou ow'st to me;
[*to Eliz.:*] And thou a kingdom;
                              [*to all:*] all of you allegiance.   170
This sorrow that I have, by right is yours,
And all the pleasures you usurp are mine.

RICHARD   The curse my noble father laid on thee,
When thou didst crown his warlike brows with paper

And with thy scorns drew'st rivers from his eyes,
And then, to dry them, gav'st the Duke a clout
Steeped in the faultless blood of pretty Rutland – [43]
His curses then, from bitterness of soul
Denounced against thee, are all fall'n upon thee;
And God, not we, hath plagued thy bloody deed.   180

Q. ELIZAB. [to Marg.:] So just is God to right the innocent.

HASTINGS   [to Marg.:] O, 'twas the foulest deed to slay that babe,[44]
And the most merciless, that e'er was heard of!

RIVERS   [to Marg.:] Tyrants themselves wept when
                                            it was reported.

DORSET   [to Marg.:] No man but prophesied revenge for it.

BUCKING.   [to Marg.:] Northumberland, then present, wept to see it.

Q. MARG.   What? Were you snarling all before I came,
Ready to catch each other by the throat,
And turn you all your hatred now on me?
Did York's dread curse prevail so much with Heaven   190
That Henry's death, my lovely Edward's death,
Their kingdom's loss, my woeful banishment,
Should all but answer for that peevish brat?
Can curses pierce the clouds and enter Heaven?
Why, then, give way, dull clouds, to my quick curses.
Though not by war, by surfeit die your King,
As ours, by murther, to make him a king!
[To Eliz.:] Edward thy son, that now is Prince of Wales,
For Edward our son, that was Prince of Wales,
Die in his youth by like untimely violence!   200
Thyself a queen, for me that was a queen,
Outlive thy glory, like my wretched self!
Long mayst thou live to wail thy children's death,
And see another, as I see thee now,
Decked in thy rights, as thou art stalled in mine!
Long die thy happy days before thy death;
And, after many lengthened hours of grief,
Die neither mother, wife, nor England's Queen!
– Rivers and Dorset, you were standers by,
– And so wast thou, Lord Hastings, –[45] when my son   210
Was stabbed with bloody daggers: God I pray Him,
That none of you may live his natural age,

But by some unlooked accident cut off!

RICHARD   Have done thy charm, thou hateful withered hag!

Q. MARG.   And leave out thee? Stay, dog, for thou shalt hear me.
If Heaven have any grievous plague in store
Exceeding those that I can wish upon thee,
O, let them keep it till thy sins be ripe,
And then hurl down their indignatiòn
On thee, the troubler of the poor world's peace!   220
The worm of conscience still begnaw thy soul!
Thy friends suspect for traitors while thou liv'st,
And take deep traitors for thy dearest friends!
No sleep close up that deadly eye of thine,
Unless it be while some tormenting dream
Affrights thee with a Hell of ugly divels!
Thou elvish-marked, abortive, rooting hog![46]
Thou that wast sealed in thy nativity
The slave of nature and the son of Hell!
Thou slander of thy heavy mother's womb!   230
Thou loathèd issue of thy father's loins!
Thou rag of honour! Thou detested –

RICHARD   Margaret.

Q. MARG.   Richard!

RICHARD   Ha?

Q. MARG.   I call thee not.

RICHARD   I cry thee mercy then, for I did think
That thou hadst called me all these bitter names.

Q. MARG.   Why, so I did, but looked for no reply.
O, let me make the period to my curse!

RICHARD   'Tis done by me, and ends in 'Margaret'.

Q. ELIZAB. [to Marg.:] Thus have you breathed your curse
                              against yourself.

Q. MARG.   Poor painted Queen, vain flourish of my fortune!   240
Why strew'st thou sugar on that bottled spider
Whose deadly web ensnareth thee about?
Fool, fool! Thou whet'st a knife to kill thyself.
The day will come that thou shalt wish for me
To help thee curse this poisonous bunch-backed toad.

HASTINGS False-boding woman, end thy frantic curse,
Lest to thy harm thou move our patìence.

Q. MARG. Foul shame upon you! You have all moved mine.

RIVERS   Were you well served, you would be taught your duty.

Q. MARG. To serve me well, you all should do me duty.   250
          Teach me to be your Queen, and you my subjects:
          O, serve me well, and teach yourselves that duty!

DORSET   Dispute not with her; she is lunatic.

Q. MARG. Peace, Master Marquis, you are malapert:
          Your fire-new stamp of honour is scarce current.[47]
          O, that your young nobility could judge
          What 'twere to lose it, and be miserable!
          They that stand high have many blasts to shake them;
          And if they fall, they dash themselves to pieces.

RICHARD   Good counsel, marry: learn it, learn it, Marquis.   260

DORSET   It touches you, my Lord, as much as me.

RICHARD   Ay, and much more; but I was born so high,
          Our eyrie buildeth in the cedar's top,
          And dallies with the wind, and scorns the sun.[48]

Q. MARG. And turns the sun to shade; alas, alas!
          Witness my son, now in the shade of death,
          Whose bright out-shining beams thy cloudy wrath
          Hath in eternal darkness folded up.
          Your eyrie buildeth in our eyrie's nest.
          O God, that seest it, do not suffer it: 270
          As it is won with blood, lost be it so!

RICHARD   Peace, peace, for shame, if not for charity.

Q. MARG. Urge neither charity nor shame to me:
          Uncharitably with me have you dealt,
          And shamefully my hopes by you are butchered.
          My charity is outrage, life my shame;
          And in that shame still live my sorrow's rage!

BUCKING. Have done, have done.

Q. MARG. O princely Buckingham, I'll kiss thy hand
          In sign of league and amity with thee: 280
          Now fair befall thee and thy noble House!
          Thy garments are not spotted with our blood,
          Nor thou within the compass of my curse.

BUCKING. Nor no one here; for curses never pass
          The lips of those that breathe them in the air.

Q. MARG. I will not think but they ascend the sky,

And there awake God's gentle-sleeping peace.
[*Aside to Buckingham, as she indicates Richard:*]
O Buckingham, take heed of yonder dog!
Look, when he fawns, he bites; and when he bites,
His venom tooth will rankle to the death.   290
Have not to do with him, beware of him;
Sin, death, and Hell have set their marks on him,
And all their ministers attend on him.

RICHARD   What doth she say, my Lord of Buckingham?
BUCKING.   Nothing that I respect, my gracious Lord.
Q. MARG.   What, dost thou scorn me for my gentle counsel,
And soothe the divel that I warn thee from?
O, but remember this another day,
When he shall split thy very heart with sorrow,
And say 'Poor Margaret was a prophetess'.   300
Live each of you the subjects to his hate,
And he to yours, and all of you to God's!   [*Exit.*

HASTINGS   My hair doth stand on end to hear her curses.⁴⁹
RIVERS   And so doth mine: I muse why she's at liberty.
RICHARD   I cannot blame her: by God's holy Mother,
She hath had too much wrong; and I repent
My part thereof that I have done to her.
Q. ELIZAB. I never did her any, to my knowledge.
RICHARD   Yet you have all the vantage of her wrong.
I was too hot to do somebody good,   310
That is too cold in thinking of it now.
Marry, as for Clarence, he is well repaid:
He is franked up to fatting for his pains.
God pardon them that are the cause thereof!
RIVERS   A virtuous and a Christian-like conclusion,
To pray for them that have done scathe to us.
RICHARD   So do I ever – [*speaks to himself:*] being well advised,
For had I cursed now, I had cursed myself.

Enter Sir William CATESBY.

CATESBY   Madam, his Majesty doth call for you,
– And for your Grace, – and you, my gracious Lords.   320
Q. ELIZAB. Catesby, I come. – Lords, will you go with me?
RIVERS   We wait upon your Grace.   [*Exeunt all but Richard.*
RICHARD   I do the wrong, and first begin to brawl.

The secret mischiefs that I set abroach
I lay unto the grievous charge of others.
Clarence, whom I indeed have cast in darkness,
I do beweep to many simple gulls,
Namely to Derby, Hastings, Buckingham;
And tell them 'tis the Queen and her allíes
That stir the King against the Duke my brother.   330
Now, they believe it; and withal whet me
To be revenged on Rivers, Dorset, Grey;
But then I sigh; and, with a piece of Scripture,
Tell them that God bids us do good for evil:
And thus I clothe my naked villainy
With odd old ends stol'n forth of Holy Writ,
And seem a saint, when most I play the Divel.

Enter TWO MURDERERS.[50]

But soft! Here come my executioners.
– How now, my hardy stout resolvèd mates:
Are you now going to dispatch this thing?   340

MURD. I We are, my Lord, and come to have the warrant,
That we may be admitted where he is.

RICHARD Well thought upon; I have it here about me.
                              [*Richard gives him the warrant.*
When you have done, repair to Crosby Place.
But, sirs, be sudden in the execution,
Withal obdúrate: do not hear him plead;
For Clarence is well–spoken, and perhaps
May move your hearts to pity, if you mark him.

MURD. 2 Tut, tut, my Lord, we will not stand to prate;
Talkers are no good doers: be assured   350
We go to use our hands, and not our tongues.

RICHARD Your eyes drop millstones, when fools' eyes fall tears.
I like you, lads: about your business straight.
Go, go, dispatch.

BOTH   We will, my noble Lord.   [*Exeunt.*

SCENE 4.

London. Inside the Tower.

Enter CLARENCE *and* BRAKENBURY.[51]

BRAKEN.   Why looks your Grace so heavily today?

CLARENCE O, I have passed a miserable night,
So full of fearful dreams, of ugly sights,
That, as I am a Christian faithful man,
I would not spend another such a night,
Though 'twere to buy a world of happy days,
So full of dismal terror was the time.

BRAKEN.   What was your dream, my Lord? I pray you, tell me.

CLARENCE Methoughts that I had broken from the Tower,
And was embarked to cross to Burgundy,   10
And in my company my brother Gloucester,
Who from my cabin tempted me to walk
Upon the hatches. Thence we looked toward England,
And cited up a thousand heavy times,
During the wars of York and Lancaster,
That had befall'n us. As we paced along
Upon the giddy footing of the hatches,
Methought that Gloucester stumbled, and in falling
Struck me (that thought to stay him) overboard,
Into the tumbling billows of the main.   20
O Lord, methought what pain it was to drown:
What dreadful noise of waters in mine ears,
What sights of ugly death within mine eyes!
Methoughts I saw a thousand fearful wracks;
Ten thousand men that fishes gnawed upon;
Wedges of gold, great anchors, heaps of pearl,[52]
Inestimable stones, unvalued jewels,
All scattered in the bottom of the sea:
Some lay in dead men's skulls; and in the holes
Where eyes did once inhabit, there were crept   30
(As 'twere in scorn of eyes) reflecting gems,
That wooed the slimy bottom of the deep,
And mocked the dead bones that lay scattered by.

BRAKEN.   Had you such leisure in the time of death

            To gaze upon these secrets of the deep?

CLARENCE Methought I had; and often did I strive
            To yield the ghost; but still the envious flood
            Stopped in my soul, and would not let it forth
            To find the empty, vast, and wand'ring air,
            But smothered it within my panting bulk,   40
            Who almost burst to belch it in the sea.

BRAKEN. Awaked you not in this sore agony?

CLARENCE No, no; my dream was lengthened after life.
            O then began the tempest to my soul!
            I passed (methought) the melancholy flood,
            With that sour ferryman which poets write of,[53]
            Unto the kingdom of perpetual night.
            The first that there did greet my stranger-soul
            Was my great father-in-law, renownèd Warwick,
            Who spake aloud, 'What scourge for perjury   50
            Can this dark monarchy afford false Clarence?',
            And so he vanished. Then came wand'ring by
            A shadow like an angel, with bright hair
            Dabbled in blood, and he shrieked out aloud,
            'Clarence is come: false, fleeting, perjured Clarence,
            That stabbed me in the field by Tewkesbury:
            Seize on him, Furies, take him unto torment!'.[54]
            With that (methought) a legion of foul fiends
            Environed me, and howled in mine ears[55]
            Such hideous cries, that with the very noise   60
            I trembling waked, and for a season after
            Could not believe but that I was in Hell,
            Such terrible impression made my dream.

BRAKEN. No marvel, Lord, though it affrighted you;
            I am afraid, methinks, to hear you tell it.

CLARENCE Ah, Keeper, Keeper, I have done these things
            (That now give evidence against my soul)
            For Edward's sake; and see how he requites me.
            – O God, if my deep prayers cannot appease Thee,
            But Thou wilt be avenged on my misdeeds,   70
            Yet execute Thy wrath in me alone:
            O spare my guiltless wife and my poor children![56]
            – Keeper, I prithee, sit by me awhile;

My soul is heavy, and I fain would sleep.
BRAKEN. I will, my Lord: God give your Grace good rest!
— Sorrow breaks seasons and reposing hours,
Makes the night morning and the noontide night.
Princes have but their titles for their glories,
An outward honour for an inward toil;
And for unfelt imaginatïons   80
They often feel a world of restless cares:
So that, between their titles and low name,
There's nothing differs but the outward fame.

Clarence sleeps. Enter the TWO MURDERERS.

MURD. I Ho! Who's here?
BRAKEN. What wouldst thou, fellow? And how cam'st
                                            thou hither?
MURD. I I would speak with Clarence, and I came hither on my
legs.
BRAKEN. What, so brief?
MURD. 2 'Tis better, sir, than to be tedious. [*To Murd. 1:*] Let him
see our commission, and talk no more.   90
                    [*Brakenbury takes the warrant and reads it.*
BRAKEN. I am in this commanded to deliver
The noble Duke of Clarence to your hands.
I will not reason what is meant hereby,
Because I will be guiltless from the meaning.
There lies the Duke asleep, and there the keys.
I'll to the King, and signify to him
That thus I have resigned to you my charge.
MURD. I You may, sir; 'tis a point of wisdom. Fare you well.
                                            [*Exit Brakenbury.*
MURD. 2 What, shall we stab him as he sleeps?
MURD. I No; he'll say 'twas done cowardly, when he wakes.   100
MURD. 2 Why, he shall never wake until the great Judgement-
Day.
MURD. I Why, then he'll say we stabbed him sleeping.
MURD. 2 The urging of that word 'Judgement' hath bred a kind
of remorse in me.
MURD. I What, art thou afraid?
MURD. 2 Not to kill him, having a warrant; but to be damned for
killing him, from the which no warrant can defend me.

MURD. I   I thought thou hadst been resolute.

MURD. 2   So I am, to let him live.   110

MURD. I   I'll back to the Duke of Gloucester, and tell him so.

MURD. 2   Nay, I prithee, stay a little: I hope this passionate humour of mine will change; it was wont to hold me but while one tells twenty.   [*Appropriate pause.*

MURD. I   How dost thou feel thyself now?

MURD. 2   Faith, some certain dregs of conscience are yet within me.

MURD. I   Remember our reward, when the deed's done.

MURD. 2   Zounds, he dies! I had forgot the reward.

MURD. I   Where's thy conscience now?   120

MURD. 2   O, in the Duke of Gloucester's purse.

MURD. I   When he opens his purse to give us our reward, thy conscience flies out.

MURD. 2   'Tis no matter, let it go; there's few or none will entertain it.

MURD. I   What if it come to thee again?

MURD. 2   I'll not meddle with it: it makes a man a coward. A man cannot steal, but it accuseth him; a man cannot swear, but it checks him; a man cannot lie with his neighbour's wife, but it detects him. 'Tis a blushing shamefaced 130 spirit, that mutinies in a man's bosom; it fills a man full of obstacles. It made me once restore a purse of gold that (by chance) I found; it beggars any man that keeps it; it is turned out of towns and cities for a dangerous thing; and every man that means to live well endeavours to trust to himself, and live without it.

MURD. I   Zounds, 'tis even now at my elbow, persuading me not to kill the Duke.

MURD. 2   Take the divel in thy mind, and believe him not: he would insinuate with thee but to make thee sigh.[57]   140

MURD. I   I am strong-framed: he cannot prevail with me.

MURD. 2   Spoke like a tall man that respects thy reputation. Come, shall we fall to work?

MURD. I   Take him on the costard with the hilts of thy sword, and then throw him into the malmsey-butt in the next room.

MURD. 2   O excellent device! And make a sop of him.

MURD. 1	Soft, he wakes.
MURD. 2	Strike!
MURD. 1	No, we'll reason with him. 150
CLARENCE	Where art thou, Keeper? Give me a cup of wine.
MURD. 1	You shall have wine enough, my Lord, anon.
CLARENCE	In God's name, what art thou?
MURD. 1	A man, as you are.
CLARENCE	But not, as I am, royal.
MURD. 1	Nor you, as we are, loyal.
CLARENCE	Thy voice is thunder, but thy looks are humble.
MURD. 1	My voice is now the King's, my looks mine own.
CLARENCE	How darkly and how deadly dost thou speak!

CLARENCE Your eyes do menace me. Why look you pale?   160
Who sent you hither? Wherefore do you come?

BOTH To, to, to –

CLARENCE To murther me?

BOTH Ay, ay.

CLARENCE You scarcely have the hearts to tell me so,
And therefore cannot have the hearts to do it.
Wherein, my friends, have I offended you?

MURD. 1 Offended us you have not, but the King.

CLARENCE I shall be reconciled to him again.

MURD. 2 Never, my Lord; therefore prepare to die.   170

CLARENCE Are you drawn forth among a world of men
To slay the innocent? What's my offence?
Where is the evidence that doth accuse me?
What lawful quest have given their verdict up
Unto the frowning judge? Or who pronounced
The bitter sentence of poor Clarence' death?
Before I be convíct by course of law,
To threaten me with death is most unlawful.
I charge you, as you hope to have redemption
By Christ's dear blood shed for our grievous sins,[58]   180
That you depart and lay no hands on me:
The deed you undertake is damnable.

MURD. 1 What we will do, we do upon command.

MURD. 2 And he that hath commanded is our King.

CLARENCE Erroneous vassals! The great King of kings
Hath in the tables of His law commanded

That thou shalt do no murther:[59] will you then
Spurn at His edict, and fulfil a man's?
Take heed; for He holds vengeance in His hand,
To hurl upon their heads that break His law.   190

MURD. 2 And that same vengeance doth He hurl on thee,
For false forswearing, and for murther too:
Thou didst receive the sacrament to fight
In quarrel of the House of Lancaster.

MURD. 1 And like a traitor to the name of God,
Didst break that vow, and with thy treacherous blade
Unrip'st the bowels of thy sov'reign's son — [60]

MURD. 2 Whom thou wast sworn to cherish and defend.

MURD. 1 How canst thou urge God's dreadful law to us,
When thou hast broke it in such dear degree?   200

CLARENCE Alas! For whose sake did I that ill deed?
For Edward, for my brother, for his sake.
He sends you not to murther me for this,
For in that sin he is as deep as I.
If God will be avengèd for the deed,
O, know you yet, he doth it publicly.
Take not the quarrel from His powerful arm:
He needs no indirect or lawless course
To cut off those that have offended Him.

MURD. 1 Who made thee then a bloody minister,   210
When gallant springing brave Plantagenet,
That princely novice, was struck dead by thee?

CLARENCE My brother's love, the Divel, and my rage.

MURD. 1 Thy brother's love, our duty, and thy faults
Provoke us hither now to slaughter thee.

CLARENCE If you do love my brother, hate not me;
I am his brother, and I love him well.
If you are hired for meed, go back again,
And I will send you to my brother Gloucester,
Who shall reward you better for my life   220
Than Edward will for tidings of my death.

MURD. 2 You are deceived: your brother Gloucester hates you.

CLARENCE O, no, he loves me, and he holds me dear:
Go you to him from me.

MURD. 1   Ay, so we will.

CLARENCE Tell him, when that our princely father York
          Blessed his three sons with his victorious arm,
          And charged us from his soul to love each other,[61]
          He little thought of this divided friendship:
          Bid Gloucester think of this, and he will weep.
MURD. I   Ay, millstones, as he lessoned us to weep.   230
CLARENCE O, do not slander him, for he is kind.
MURD. I   Right, as snow in harvest. Come, you deceive yourself:
          'Tis he that sends us to destroy you here.
CLARENCE It cannot be; for he bewept my fortune,
          And hugged me in his arms, and swore with sobs
          That he would labour my delivery.
MURD. I   Why, so he doth, when he delivers you
          From this earth's thraldom to the joys of Heaven.
MURD. 2   Make peace with God, for you must die, my Lord.
CLARENCE Have you that holy feeling in your souls,   240
          To counsel me to make my peace with God,
          And are you yet to your own souls so blind
          That you will war with God by murth'ring me?
          O, sirs, consider, they that set you on
          To do this deed will hate you for the deed.
MURD. 2   What shall we do?
CLARENCE   Relent, and save your souls.
          Which of you, if you were a prince's son,
          Being pent from liberty, as I am now,
          If two such murtherers as yourselves came to you,
          Would not entreat for life? As you would beg,   250
          Were you in my distress.[62]
MURD. I   'Relent'? No, 'tis cowardly and womanish.
CLARENCE Not to relent is beastly, savage, divelish.
          [To Murd. 2:] My friend, I spy some pity in thy looks:
          O, if thine eye be not a flatterer,
          Come thou on my side, and entreat for me:
          A begging prince, what beggar pities not?
MURD. 2   Look behind you, my Lord.   [Clarence turns.
MURD. I   [stabs Clarence:] Take that, and that! If all this will not do,
          I'll drown you in the malmsey-butt within.   260
                                              [Exit with the body.
MURD. 2   A bloody deed, and desp'rately dispatched:

How fain, like Pilate, would I wash my hands
Of this most grievous murther!

Enter MURDERER 1.

MURD. 1 How now? What mean'st thou, that thou help'st
me not?
By Heaven, the Duke shall know how slack you
have been.

MURD. 2 I would he knew that I had saved his brother.
Take thou the fee, and tell him what I say,
For I repent me that the Duke is slain.   [*Exit.*

MURD. 1 So do not I: go, coward as thou art.
– Well, I'll go hide the body in some hole,   270
Till that the Duke give order for his burial;
And when I have my meed, I will away;
For this will out, and then I must not stay.   [*Exit.*

ACT 2, SCENE I.

London. The Palace.

Flourish. Enter KING EDWARD, *sick, with*
QUEEN ELIZABETH, DORSET, RIVERS, HASTINGS,
BUCKINGHAM, GREY, *and* OTHERS.

K. EDWARD Why, so: now have I done a good day's work.
You peers, continue this united league:
I every day expect an embassage
From my Redeemer to redeem me hence;[63]
And more at peace my soul shall part to Heaven,
Since I have made my friends at peace on earth.
Hastings and Rivers, take each other's hand:
Dissemble not your hatred; swear your love.

RIVERS By Heaven, my soul is purged from grudging hate,
And with my hand I seal my true heart's love.   10

HASTINGS So thrive I, as I truly swear the like!
                                        [*They clasp hands.*

K. EDWARD Take heed you dally not before your King;
Lest he that is the supreme King of kings
Confound your hidden falsehood, and award
Either of you to be the other's end.

HASTINGS So prosper I, as I swear perfect love!

RIVERS And I, as I love Hastings with my heart!

K. EDWARD [*to Eliz.:*] Madam, yourself is not exempt from this,
– Nor you, son Dorset; – Buckingham, nor you:
You have been factious one against the other. –   20
Wife, love Lord Hastings: let him kiss your hand;
And what you do, do it unfeignèdly.
                            [*She offers her hand; Hastings kisses it.*

Q. ELIZAB. There, Hastings; I will never more remember
Our former hatred, so thrive I and mine!

K. EDWARD Dorset, embrace him; – Hastings, love Lord Marquis.

DORSET This interchange of love, I here protest,
Upon my part shall be inviolable.

HASTINGS And so swear I.   [*They embrace.*

K. EDWARD Now, princely Buckingham, seal thou this league

With thy embracements to my wife's allies, 30
And make me happy in your unity.

BUCKING. [*to Eliz.:*] Whenever Buckingham doth turn his hate
Upon your Grace, nor with all duteous love
Doth cherish you and yours, God punish me
With hate in those where I expect most love!
When I have most need to employ a friend,
And most assured that he is a friend,[64]
Deep, hollow, treacherous and full of guile
Be he unto me! This do I beg of God,
When I am cold in love to you or yours. [*They embrace.* 40

K. EDWARD A pleasing cordial, princely Buckingham,
Is this thy vow unto my sickly heart.
There wanteth now our brother Gloucester here,
To make the blessèd period of this peace.

BUCKING. And in good time,
Here comes Sir Richard Ratcliffe and the Duke.

Enter RICHARD *and Sir Richard* RATCLIFFE.

RICHARD Good morrow to my sovereign King and Queen;
– And, princely peers, a happy time of day!

K. EDWARD Happy indeed, as we have spent the day.
Gloucester, we have done deeds of charity, 50
Made peace of enmity, fair love of hate,
Between these swelling wrong-incensèd peers.

RICHARD A blessèd labour, my most sovereign Lord.
Among this princely heap, if any here,
By false intelligence or wrong surmise,
Hold me a foe,
If I unwittingly, or in my rage,
Have aught committed that is hardly borne
By any in this presence, I desire
To reconcile me to his friendly peace: 60
'Tis death to me to be at enmity;
I hate it, and desire all good men's love.
– First, madam, I entreat true peace of you,
Which I will purchase with my duteous service;
– Of you, my noble cousin Buckingham,
If ever any grudge were lodged between us;

	– Of you, Lord Rivers, and Lord Grey of you,[65]	
	That all without desert have frowned on me; –	
	Dukes, Earls, Lords, gentlemen; indeed, of all.	
	I do not know that Englishman alive	70
	With whom my soul is any jot at odds	
	More than the infant that is born tonight.	
	I thank my God for my humility.	
Q. ELIZAB.	A holy day shall this be kept hereafter:	
	I would to God all strifes were well compounded.	
	– My sovereign Lord, I do beseech your Highness	
	To take our brother Clarence to your grace.	
RICHARD	Why, madam, have I offered love for this,	
	To be so flouted in this royal presence?	
	Who knows not that the gentle Duke is dead?	80

[They all evince shock.

	You do him injury to scorn his corse.
RIVERS	Who knows not he is dead? Who knows he *is*?
Q. ELIZAB.	All-seeing Heaven, what a world is this!
BUCKING.	Look I so pale, Lord Dorset, as the rest?
DORSET	Ay, my good Lord, and no man in the presence
	But his red colour hath forsook his cheeks.
K. EDWARD	Is Clarence dead? The order was reversed.
RICHARD	But he (poor man) by your first order died,

	And that a wingèd Mercury did bear;[66]	
	Some tardy cripple bore the countermand	90
	That came too lag to see him burièd.	
	God grant that some, less noble and less loyal,	
	Nearer in bloody thoughts, but not in blood,	
	Deserve not worse than wretched Clarence did,	
	And yet go current from suspiciòn![67]	

Enter STANLEY.

STANLEY	[*to King:*] A boon, my sovereign, for my service done!	

[He kneels.

K. EDWARD	I prithee, peace: my soul is full of sorrow.	
STANLEY	I will not rise, unless your Highness hear me.	
K. EDWARD	Then say at once what is it thou demand'st.	
STANLEY	The forfeit, sovereign, of my servant's life,[68]	100
	Who slew today a riotous gentleman	

Lately attendant on the Duke of Norfolk.

K. EDWARD Have I a tongue to doom my brother's death,
And shall that tongue give pardon to a slave?
My brother killed no man; his fault was thought,
And yet his punishment was bitter death.
Who sued to me for him? Who (in my wrath)
Kneeled at my feet and bid me be advised?
Who spoke of brotherhood? Who spoke of love?
Who told me how the poor soul did forsake   110
The mighty Warwick, and did fight for me?
Who told me, in the field at Tewkesbury
When Oxford had me down, he rescued me
And said 'Dear brother, live, and be a king'?
Who told me, when we both lay in the field
Frozen almost to death, how he did lap me
Even in his garments, and did give himself
(All thin and naked) to the numb-cold night?
All this from my remembrance brutish wrath
Sinfully plucked, and not a man of you   120
Had so much grace to put it in my mind.
But when your carters or your waiting-vassals
Have done a drunken slaughter, and defaced
The precious image of our dear Redeemer,
You straight are on your knees for pardon, pardon;
– And I, unjustly too, must grant it you.   [*Stanley rises.*
– But for my brother not a man would speak,
Nor I, ungracious, speak unto myself
For him, poor soul. The proudest of you all
Have been beholding to him in his life;   130
Yet none of you would once beg for his life,
– O God, I fear Thy justice will take hold
On me, and you, and mine, and yours, for this!
– Come, Hastings, help me to my closet. Ah,
Poor Clarence!
              [*Exit the King, helped by Hastings, and attended
                         by the Queen, Rivers and Dorset.*

RICHARD This is the fruits of rashness. Marked you not
How that the guilty kindred of the Queen
Looked pale when they did hear of Clarence' death?

O, they did urge it still unto the King:
God will revenge it. Come, Lords, will you go   140
To comfort Edward with our company?

BUCKING. We wait upon your Grace.   [*Exeunt.*

SCENE 2.

London. The Palace.

Enter the old DUCHESS OF YORK
with the TWO CHILDREN OF CLARENCE.

BOY   Good grandam, tell us, is our father dead?
DUCHESS   No, boy.
GIRL   Why do you weep so oft, and beat your breast,
          And cry 'O Clarence, my unhappy son!'?
BOY   Why do you look on us, and shake your head,
          And call us 'orphans', 'wretches', 'castaways',
          If that our noble father were alive?
DUCHESS   My pretty cousins, you mistake me both.
          I do lament the sickness of the King,
          As loath to lose him, not your father's death: 10
          It were lost sorrow to wail one that's lost.
BOY   Then you conclude, my grandam, he is dead.
          The King mine uncle is to blame for it.
          God will revenge it, Whom I will importune
          With earnest prayers, all to that effect.
GIRL   And so will I.
DUCHESS   Peace, children, peace! The King doth love you well.
          Incapable and shallow innocents,
          You cannot guess who caused your father's death.
BOY   Grandam, we can; for my good uncle Gloucester   20
          Told me the King, provoked to it by the Queen,
          Devised impeachments to imprison him;
          And when my uncle told me so, he wept,
          And pitied me, and kindly kissed my cheek;
          Bade me rely on him as on my father,
          And he would love me dearly as a child.
DUCHESS   Ah, that deceit should steal such gentle shape,
          And with a virtuous visor hide deep vice!

He is my son, ay, and therein my shame;
Yet from my dugs he drew not this deceit.   30

BOY   Think you my uncle did dissemble, grandam?
DUCHESS   Ay, boy.
BOY   I cannot think it. – Hark! What noise is this?

Enter QUEEN ELIZABETH *dishevelled, wailing,*
followed by RIVERS *and* DORSET.[69]

Q. ELIZAB.   Ah, who shall hinder me to wail and weep,
             To chide my fortune and torment myself?
             I'll join with black despair against my soul,
             And to myself become an enemy.
DUCHESS   What means this scene of rude impatiènce?
Q. ELIZAB.   To mark an act of tragic violence.
             Edward, my Lord, thy son, our King, is dead.[70]   40
             Why grow the branches when the root is gone?
             Why wither not the leaves that want their sap?
             If you will live, lament; if die, be brief,
             That our swift-wingèd souls may catch the King's,
             Or, like obedient subjects, follow him
             To his new kingdom of ne'er-changing night.
DUCHESS   Ah, so much interest have I in thy sorrow
             As I had title in thy noble husband.
             I have bewept a worthy husband's death,
             And lived with looking on his images;   50
             But now two mirrors of his princely semblance[71]
             Are cracked in pieces by malignant death,
             And I for comfort have but one false glass,
             That grieves me when I see my shame in him.
             Thou art a widow; yet thou art a mother,
             And hast the comfort of thy children left;
             But death hath snatched my husband from mine arms,
             And plucked two crutches from my feeble hands,
             Clarence and Edward. O, what cause have I,
             Thine being but a moiety of my moan,   60
             To overgo thy woes and drown thy cries!
BOY   [*to Eliz.:*] Ah, aunt! You wept not for our father's death:
             How can we aid you with our kindred tears?
GIRL   [*to Eliz.:*] Our fatherless distress was left unmoaned:
             Your widow-dolour likewise be unwept!

Q. ELIZAB. Give me no help in lamentatiòn;
            I am not barren to bring forth complaints:
            All springs reduce their currents to mine eyes,
            That I, being governed by the wat'ry moon,
            May send forth plenteous tears to drown the world!   70
            Ah, for my husband, for my dear Lord Edward!
CHILDREN   Ah, for our father, for our dear Lord Clarence!
DUCHESS   Alas for both, both mine, Edward and Clarence!
Q. ELIZAB. What stay had I but Edward? And he's gone.
CHILDREN   What stay had we but Clarence? And he's gone.
DUCHESS   What stays had I but they? And they are gone.
Q. ELIZAB. Was never widow had so dear a loss.
CHILDREN   Were never orphans had so dear a loss.
DUCHESS   Was never mother had so dear a loss.
            Alas, I am the mother of these griefs!   80
            Their woes are parcelled, mine is general.
            She for an Edward weeps, and so do I;
            I for a Clarence weep, so doth not she:
            These babes for Clarence weep, and so do I;
            I for an Edward weep, so do not they.
            Alas, you three on me, threefold distressed,
            Pour all your tears: I am your sorrow's nurse,
            And I will pamper it with lamentation.
DORSET   Comfort, dear mother: God is much displeased
            That you take with unthankfulness His doing.   90
            In common worldly things, 'tis called ungrateful,
            With dull unwillingness to repay a debt
            Which with a bounteous hand was kindly lent;
            Much more to be thus opposite with Heaven
            For it requires the royal debt it lent you.
RIVERS   Madam, bethink you, like a careful mother,
            Of the young Prince your son. Send straight for him;
            Let him be crowned; in him your comfort lives.
            Drown desperate sorrow in dead Edward's grave,
            And plant your joys in living Edward's throne.[72]   100

            Enter RICHARD, BUCKINGHAM, STANLEY,
                  HASTINGS *and* RATCLIFFE.

RICHARD   Sister, have comfort: all of us have cause
            To wail the dimming of our shining star,

But none can help our harms by wailing them.
– Madam, my mother, I do cry you mercy;
I did not see your Grace. Humbly on my knee
I crave your blessing.   [*He kneels.*

DUCHESS God bless thee, and put meekness in thy breast,
Love, charity, obedience, and true duty.

RICHARD Amen! [*He rises; aside:*] And make me die a good
                                    old man!
That is the butt-end of a mother's blessing: 110
I marvel that her Grace did leave it out.

BUCKING. You cloudy princes and heart-sorrowing peers
That bear this heavy mutual load of moan,
Now cheer each other in each other's love.
Though we have spent our harvest of this King,
We are to reap the harvest of his son.
The broken rancour of your high-swoll'n hearts,
But lately splinted, knit, and joined together,[73]
Must gently be preserved, cherished, and kept:
Meseemeth good that, with some little train,   120
Forthwith from Ludlow the young Prince be fet[74]
Hither to London, to be crowned our King.

RIVERS Why with some *little* train, my Lord of Buckingham?

BUCKING. Marry, my Lord, lest by a multitude
The new-healed wound of malice should break out;
Which would be so much the more dangerous,
By how much the estate is green and yet ungoverned.
Where every horse bears his commanding rein,
And may direct his course as please himself,
As well the fear of harm, as harm apparent,   130
In my opinion, ought to be prevented.

RICHARD I hope the King made peace with all of us;
And the compáct is firm and true in me.

RIVERS And so in me; and so (I think) in all.
Yet, since it is but green, it should be put
To no apparent likelihood of breach,
Which haply by much company might be urged:
Therefore I say with noble Buckingham
That it is meet so few should fetch the Prince.

HASTINGS And so say I.[75]   140

RICHARD   Then be it so; and go we to determine
           Who they shall be that straight shall post to Ludlow.
           – Madam, and you, my sister, will you go
           To give your censures in this business?

Q. ELIZAB. ⎫
           ⎬ With all our hearts.
DUCHESS   ⎭

                              [*Exeunt all but Buckingham and Richard.*

BUCKING.   My Lord, whoever journeys to the Prince,
           For God's sake let not us two stay at home;
           For by the way I'll sort occasion,
           As index to the story we late talked of,
           To part the Queen's proud kindred from the Prince.   150

RICHARD   My other self, my counsel's consistory,
           My oracle, my prophet, my dear cousin:
           I, as a child, will go by thy direction.
           Toward Ludlow then, for we'll not stay behind.

                                                    [*Exeunt.*

SCENE 3.

London. A street.

Enter TWO CITIZENS, *meeting.*

CITIZEN 1   Good morrow, neighbour: whither away so fast?
CITIZEN 2   I promise you, I scarcely know myself:
            Hear you the news abroad?
CITIZEN 1   Yes, that the King is dead.
CITIZEN 2   Ill news, by'r Lady. Seldom comes the better.
            I fear, I fear, 'twill prove a giddy world.

Enter another CITIZEN.

CITIZEN 3   Neighbours, God speed!
CITIZEN 1   Give you good morrow, sir.
CITIZEN 3   Doth the news hold of good King Edward's death?
CITIZEN 2   Ay, sir, it is too true, God help the while!
CITIZEN 3   Then, masters, look to see a troublous world.
CITIZEN 1   No, no; by God's good grace, his son shall reign.   10
CITIZEN 3   Woe to that land that's governed by a child!
CITIZEN 2   In him there is a hope of government,

Which, in his nonage, council under him,
And, in his full and ripened years, himself,
No doubt shall then, and till then, govern well.

CITIZEN 1 So stood the state when Henry the Sixth
Was crowned in Paris but at nine months old.

CITIZEN 3 Stood the state so? No, no, good friends, God wot;
For then this land was famously enriched
With politic grave counsel; then the King   20
Had virtuous uncles to protect his Grace.

CITIZEN 1 Why, so hath this, both by his father and mother.

CITIZEN 3 Better it were they all came by his father,
Or by his father there were none at all;
For emulation who shall now be nearest
Will touch us all too near, if God prevent not.
O full of danger is the Duke of Gloucester,
And the Queen's sons and brothers haught and proud;
And were they to be ruled, and not to rule,
This sickly land might solace as before.   30

CITIZEN 1 Come, come, we fear the worst; all will be well.

CITIZEN 3 When clouds are seen, wise men put on their cloaks;
When great leaves fall, then winter is at hand;
When the sun sets, who doth not look for night?
Untimely storms makes men expect a dearth.
All may be well; but, if God sort it so,
'Tis more than we deserve, or I expect.

CITIZEN 2 Truly, the hearts of men are full of fear:
You cannot reason almost with a man
That looks not heavily and full of dread.   40

CITIZEN 3 Before the days of change, still is it so:
By a divine instínct men's minds mistrust
Ensuing danger, as by proof we see
The water swell before a boist'rous storm.
But leave it all to God. Whither away?

CITIZEN 2 Marry, we were sent for to the Justices.

CITIZEN 3 And so was I: I'll bear you company.   [Exeunt.

SCENE 4.

London. The Palace.

Enter the ARCHBISHOP OF YORK, *the young* DUKE OF YORK, QUEEN
ELIZABETH *and the old* DUCHESS OF YORK.

ARCHB.	Last night, I hear, they lay at Stony Stratford,
	And at Northampton they do rest tonight:
	Tomorrow, or next day, they will be here,
DUCHESS	I long with all my heart to see the Prince:
	I hope he is much grown since last I saw him.
Q. ELIZAB.	But I hear, no; they say my son of York
	Has almost overtane him in his growth.[76]
YORK	Ay, mother, but I would not have it so.
DUCHESS	Why, my good cousin, it is good to grow.
YORK	Grandam, one night, as we did sit at supper, 10
	My uncle Rivers talked how I did grow
	More than my brother. 'Ay,' quoth my uncle
	Gloucester,
	'Small herbs have grace; great weeds do grow apace'.
	And since, methinks I would not grow so fast,
	Because sweet flowers are slow and weeds make haste.
DUCHESS	Good faith, good faith, the saying did not hold
	In him that did object the same to thee:
	He was the wretched'st thing when he was young,
	So long a-growing and so leisurely,
	That, if his rule were true, he should be gracious. 20
ARCHB.	And so, no doubt, he is, my gracious madam.[77]
DUCHESS	I hope he is, but yet let mothers doubt.
YORK	Now, by my troth, if I had been remembered,
	I could have given my uncle's Grace a flout,
	To touch his growth nearer than he touched mine.[78]
DUCHESS	How, my young York? I prithee, let me hear it.
YORK	Marry, they say my uncle grew so fast
	That he could gnaw a crust at two hours old;
	'Twas full two years ere I could get a tooth.
	Grandam, this would have been a biting jest. 30
DUCHESS	I prithee, pretty York, who told thee this?
YORK	Grandam, his nurse.

DUCHESS   His nurse! Why, she was dead ere thou wast born.
YORK   If 'twere not she, I cannot tell who told me.
Q. ELIZAB. A parlous boy: go to, you are too shrewd.
DUCHESS   Good madam, be not angry with the child.[79]
Q. ELIZAB. Pitchers have ears.[80]

Enter a MESSENGER.[81]

ARCHB.   Here comes a messenger. – What news?
MESSENGER Such news, my Lord, as grieves me to report.
Q. ELIZAB. How doth the Prince?
MESSENGER   Well, madam, and in health.   40
DUCHESS   What is thy news?
MESSENGER   Lord Rivers and Lord Grey
           Are sent to Pomfret, and with them
           Sir Thomas Vaughan, prisoners.[82]
DUCHESS   Who hath committed them?
MESSENGER   The mighty Dukes,
           Gloucester and Buckingham.
ARCHB.   For what offence?
MESSENGER The sum of all I can, I have disclosed.
           Why or for what the nobles were committed
           Is all unknown to me, my gracious Lord.
Q. ELIZAB. Ay me, I see the ruin of my house!
           The tiger now hath seized the gentle hind;   50
           Insulting tyranny begins to jet[83]
           Upon the innocent and aweless throne:
           Welcome, destruction, blood, and massacre!
           I see (as in a map) the end of all.
DUCHESS   Accursèd and unquiet wrangling days,
           How many of you have mine eyes beheld?
           My husband lost his life to get the crown;
           And often up and down my sons were tossed,
           For me to joy and weep their gain and loss;
           And being seated, and domestic broils   60
           Clean overblown, themselves, the conquerors,
           Make war upon themselves, brother to brother,
           Blood to blood, self to self! Preposterous
           And frantic outrage, end thy damnèd spleen;
           Or let me die, to look on death no more![84]

Q. ELIZAB.   [*to York:*] Come, come, my boy: we will to sanctuary.[85]
             – Madam, farewell.
DUCHESS   Stay, I will go with you.
Q. ELIZAB.   You have no cause.
ARCHB.   [*to Eliz.:*]   My gracious lady, go;
             And thither bear your treasure and your goods.
             For my part, I'll resign unto your Grace   70
             The Seal I keep;[86] and so betide to me
             As well I tender you and all of yours!
             Go; I'll conduct you to the sanctuary.   [*Exeunt.*

ACT 3, SCENE I.[87]

London. A street.

Trumpets sound. Enter the young PRINCE EDWARD *(the uncrowned King),* GLOUCESTER *and* BUCKINGHAM, *the Lord* CARDINAL, STANLEY, CATESBY *and* OTHERS.

BUCKING.	Welcome, sweet Prince, to London, to your Chamber.[88]
RICHARD	Welcome, dear cousin, my thoughts' sovereign.
	The weary way hath made you melancholy.
PRINCE	No, uncle; but our crosses on the way
	Have made it tedious, wearisome, and heavy.
	I want more uncles here to welcome me.
RICHARD	Sweet Prince, the untainted virtue of your years
	Hath not yet dived into the world's deceit;
	Nor more can you distinguish of a man
	Than of his outward show, which, God He knows, 10
	Seldom or never jumpeth with the heart.
	Those uncles which you want were dangerous;[89]
	Your Grace attended to their sugared words,
	But looked not on the poison of their hearts.
	God keep you from them, and from such false friends!
PRINCE	God keep me from false friends; but they were none.
RICHARD	My Lord, the Mayor of London comes to greet you.

Enter the LORD MAYOR *with* ATTENDANTS.

MAYOR	God bless your Grace with health and happy days!
PRINCE	I thank you, good my Lord, and thank you all.
	I thought my mother and my brother York 20
	Would long ere this have met us on the way.
	Fie, what a slug is Hastings, that he comes not
	To tell us whether they will come or no.

Enter HASTINGS.

BUCKING.	And, in good time, here comes the sweating Lord.
PRINCE	Welcome, my Lord. What, will our mother come?
HASTINGS	On what occasion, God He knows, not I,
	The Queen your mother and your brother York
	Have taken sanctuary. The tender Prince

           Would fain have come with me to meet your Grace,
           But by his mother was perforce withheld.   30

BUCKING.   Fie, what an indirect and peevish course
           Is this of hers! – Lord Cardinal, will your Grace
           Persuade the Queen to send the Duke of York
           Unto his princely brother presently?
           – If she deny, Lord Hastings, go with him,
           And from her jealous arms pluck him perforce.

CARDINAL   My Lord of Buckingham, if my weak oratory
           Can from his mother win the Duke of York,
           Anon expect him here; but if she be obdúrate
           To mild entreaties, God in Heaven forbid   40
           We should infringe the holy privilege
           Of blessèd sanctuary! Not for all this land
           Would I be guilty of so deep a sin.

BUCKING.   You are too senseless-obstinate, my Lord,
           Too ceremonious and traditional.
           Weigh it but with the grossness of this age,
           You break not sanctuary in seizing him:
           The benefit thereof is always granted
           To those whose dealings have deserved the place,
           And those who have the wit to claim the place.   50
           This Prince hath neither claimed it nor deserved it;
           And therefore, in mine opinion, cannot have it.
           Then, taking him from thence that is not there,
           You break no privilege nor charter there.
           Oft have I heard of sanctuary *men*,
           But sanctuary *children* ne'er till now.

CARDINAL   My Lord, you shall o'er-rule my mind for once.
           – Come on, Lord Hastings, will you go with me?

HASTINGS   I go, my Lord.

PRINCE   Good Lords, make all the speedy haste you may.   60
                        [*Exeunt Cardinal and Hastings.*
           – Say, uncle Gloucester, if our brother come,
           Where shall we sojourn till our coronation?

RICHARD   Where it seems best unto your royal self.
           If I may counsel you, some day or two
           Your Highness shall repose you at the Tower;
           Then where you please, and shall be thought most fit

	For your best health and recreatiòn.
PRINCE	I do not like the Tower, of any place.
	– Did Julius Caesar build that place, my Lord?[90]
BUCKING.	He did, my gracious Lord, begin that place,
	Which, since, succeeding ages have re-edified.
PRINCE	Is it upon recórd, or else reported
	Successively from age to age, he built it?
BUCKING.	Upon recórd, my gracious lord.
PRINCE	But say, my Lord, it were not registered,
	Methinks the truth should live from age to age,
	As 'twere retailed to all posterity,
	Even to the general All-ending Day.
RICHARD	[aside:] So wise so young, they say, do ne'er live long.
PRINCE	What say you, uncle?
RICHARD	I say, without charácters, fame lives long.
	[Aside] Thus, like the formal Vice, Iniquity,
	I moralise two meanings in one word.[91]
PRINCE	That Julius Caesar was a famous man:
	With what his valour did enrich his wit,
	His wit set down to make his valour live.[92]
	Death makes no conquest of this conqueror,
	For now he lives in fame, though not in life.
	– I'll tell you what, my cousin Buckingham.
BUCKING.	What, my gracious Lord?
PRINCE	And if I live until I be a man,
	I'll win our ancient right in France again,[93]
	Or die a soldier, as I lived a king.
RICHARD	[aside:] Short summers lightly have a forward spring.[94]

Enter the young Duke of YORK, HASTINGS *and the* CARDINAL.

BUCKING.	Now, in good time, here comes the Duke of York.
PRINCE	Richard of York! How fares our loving brother?
YORK	Well, my dread Lord: so must I call you now.
PRINCE	Ay, brother, to our grief, as it is yours:
	Too late he died that might have kept that title,
	Which by his death hath lost much majesty.
RICHARD	How fares our cousin, noble Lord of York?
YORK	I thank you, gentle uncle. O, my Lord,
	You said that idle weeds are fast in growth:
	The Prince, my brother, hath outgrown me far.

Line numbers: 70, 80, 90, 100

RICHARD   He hath, my Lord.

YORK   And therefore is he idle?

RICHARD   O my fair cousin, I must not say so.

YORK   Then he is more beholding to you than I.

RICHARD   He may command me as my sovereign,
             But you have power in me as in a kinsman.

YORK   I pray you, uncle, give me this dagger.   110

RICHARD   My dagger, little cousin? With all my heart.

PRINCE   A beggar, brother?

YORK   Of my kind uncle, that I know will give,
             It being but a toy, which is no grief to give.[95]

RICHARD   A greater gift than that I'll give my cousin.

YORK   A greater gift? O, that's the sword to it.

RICHARD   Ay, gentle cousin, were it light enough.

YORK   O then, I see, you will part but with light gifts;
             In weightier things you'll say a beggar nay.

RICHARD   It is too heavy for your Grace to wear.   120

YORK   I'd weigh it lightly, were it heavier.[96]

RICHARD   What, would you have my weapon, little Lord?

YORK   I would, that I might thank you as you call me.

RICHARD   How?

YORK   Little.

PRINCE   My Lord of York will still be cross in talk:
             Uncle, your Grace knows how to bear with him.

YORK   You mean, to bear me, not to bear with me.
             Uncle, my brother mocks both you and me:
             Because that I am little, like an ape,   130
             He thinks that you should bear me on your shoulders.[97]

BUCKING.   With what a sharp-provided wit he reasons!
             To mitigate the scorn he gives his uncle,
             He prettily and aptly taunts himself:
             So cunning and so young is wonderful.

RICHARD   [to Prince:] My Lord, will't please you pass along?
             Myself and my good cousin Buckingham
             Will to your mother, to entreat of her
             To meet you at the Tower and welcome you.

YORK   What, will you go unto the Tower, my Lord?   140

PRINCE   My Lord Protector needs will have it so.

YORK   I shall not sleep in quiet at the Tower.

RICHARD   Why, what should you fear?
YORK   Marry, my uncle Clarence' angry ghost:
          My grandam told me he was murthered there.
PRINCE   I fear no uncles dead.
RICHARD   Nor none that live, I hope.
PRINCE   And if they live, I hope I need not fear.
          But come, my Lord; and with a heavy heart,
          Thinking on them, go I unto the Tower.   150
                      [*A sennet. Exeunt all but Richard,*
                                 Buckingham and Catesby.

BUCKING. [*to Richard:*] Think you, my Lord, this little prating York
          Was not incensèd by his subtle mother
          To taunt and scorn you thus opprobriously?
RICHARD   No doubt, no doubt. O 'tis a perilous boy;
          Bold, quick, ingenious, forward, capable:
          He is all the mother's, from the top to toe.
BUCKING. Well, let them rest. – Come hither, Catesby: thou
          Art sworn as deeply t'effect what we intend,[98]
          As closely to conceal what we impart:
          Thou know'st our reasons urged upon the way.   160
          What think'st thou? Is it not an easy matter
          To make Lord William Hastings of our mind,
          For the instalment of this noble Duke
          In the seat royal of this famous isle?
CATESBY   He for his father's sake so loves the Prince
          That he will not be won to aught against him.
BUCKING. What think'st thou then of Stanley? Will not he?
CATESBY   He will do all in all as Hastings doth.
BUCKING. Well, then, no more but this: go, gentle Catesby,
          And, as it were far off, sound thou Lord Hastings   170
          How he doth stand affected to our purpose,
          And summon him tomorrow to the Tower,
          To sit about the coronatiòn.
          If thou dost find him tractable to us,
          Encourage him, and tell him all our reasons;[99]
          If he be leaden, icy-cold, unwilling,
          Be thou so too, and so break off the talk,
          And give us notice of his inclination:
          For we tomorrow hold divided Councils,[100]

Wherein thyself shalt highly be employed.   180

RICHARD   Commend me to Lord William: tell him, Catesby,
His ancient knot of dangerous advers'ries
Tomorrow are let blood at Pomfret Castle;
And bid my Lord, for joy of this good news,
Give Mistress Shore one gentle kiss the more.[101]

BUCKING.   Good Catesby, go effect this business soundly.

CATESBY   My good Lords both, with all the heed I can.

RICHARD   Shall we hear from you, Catesby, ere we sleep?

CATESBY   You shall, my Lord.

RICHARD   At Crosby House, there shall you find us both.   190

[Exit Catesby.

BUCKING.   My Lord, what shall we do, if we perceive
Lord Hastings will not yield to our complots?

RICHARD   Chop off his head: something we will determine.[102]
And look when I am King, claim thou of me
The Earldom of Hereford, and all the movables
Whereof the King my brother was possessed.

BUCKING.   I'll claim that promise at your Grace's hand.

RICHARD   And look to have it yielded with all kindness.
Come, let us sup betimes, that afterwards
We may digest our complots in some form.[103] [Exeunt.   200

SCENE 2.

London. Outside Lord Hastings' house. Night.

Enter a MESSENGER, *who approaches the door.*

MESSENGER [*knocking:*] My Lord! My Lord!

HASTINGS   [*within:*] Who knocks?

MESSENGER One from the Lord Stanley.

HASTINGS   [*within:*] What is't o'clock?

MESSENGER Upon the stroke of four.

Opening the door, HASTINGS *enters from within.*

HASTINGS   Cannot my Lord Stanley sleep these tedious nights?

MESSENGER So it appears by that I have to say.
First, he commends him to your noble self.

HASTINGS   What then?

MESSENGER Then certifies your Lordship that this night   10
           He dreamt the boar had razèd off his helm;[104]
           Besides, he says there are two Councils kept;
           And that may be determined at the one
           Which may make you and him to rue at th'other.
           Therefore he sends to know your Lordship's pleasure:
           If you will presently take horse with him,
           And with all speed post with him toward the north,
           To shun the danger that his soul divines.
HASTINGS   Go, fellow, go, return unto thy Lord;
           Bid him not fear the separated Councils: 20
           His Honour and myself are at the one;
           And at the other is my good friend Catesby,
           Where nothing can proceed that toucheth us
           Whereof I shall not have intelligence.
           Tell him his fears are shallow, without instance;
           And for his dreams, I wonder he's so simple
           To trust the mock'ry of unquiet slumbers.
           To fly the boar before the boar pursues
           Were to incense the boar to follow us
           And make pursuit where he did mean no chase.   30
           Go, bid thy master rise and come to me,
           And we will both together to the Tower,
           Where he shall see the boar will use us kindly.
MESSENGER I'll go, my Lord, and tell him what you say.   [*Exit.*

                    Enter CATESBY.

CATESBY   Many good morrows to my noble Lord!
HASTINGS   Good morrow, Catesby. You are early stirring:
           What news, what news, in this our tott'ring state?
CATESBY   It is a reeling world indeed, my Lord;
           And I believe will never stand upright
           Till Richard wear the garland of the realm.   40
HASTINGS   How, 'wear the garland'? Dost thou mean the crown?
CATESBY   Ay, my good Lord.
HASTINGS   I'll have this crown of mine cut from my shoulders
           Before I'll see the crown so foul misplaced.
           But canst thou guess that he doth aim at it?
CATESBY   Ay, on my life, and hopes to find you forward

Upon his party for the gain thereof;
And thereupon he sends you this good news,
That this same very day your enemies,
The kindred of the Queen, must die at Pomfret.   50

HASTINGS   Indeed, I am no mourner for that news,
Because they have been still my advers'ries;
But, that I'll give my voice on Richard's side,
To bar my master's heirs in true descent,
God knows I will not do it, to the death.

CATESBY   God keep your Lordship in that gracious mind!

HASTINGS   But I shall laugh at this a twelvemonth hence,
That they which brought me in my master's hate,[105]
I live to look upon their tragedy.
Well, Catesby, ere a fortnight make me older,   60
I'll send some packing that yet think not on't.

CATESBY   'Tis a vile thing to die, my gracious Lord,
When men are unprepared and look not for it.

HASTINGS   O monstrous, monstrous! And so falls it out
With Rivers, Vaughan, Grey; and so 'twill do
With some men else, that think themselves as safe
As thou and I, who, as thou know'st, are dear
To princely Richard and to Buckingham.

CATESBY   The Princes both make high account of you –
[aside:] For they account his head upon the Bridge.[106]   70

HASTINGS   I know they do, and I have well deserved it.

Enter STANLEY.

[To Stanley:] Come on, come on, where is your boar-
                                                   spear, man?
Fear you the boar, and go so unprovided?

STANLEY   My Lord, good morrow; – good morrow, Catesby.
[To Hastings:] You may jest on, but, by the Holy Rood,
I do not like these several Councils, I.

HASTINGS   My Lord, I hold my life as dear as yours,
And never in my days, I do protest,
Was it so precious to me as 'tis now:
Think you, but that I know our state secure,   80
I would be so triumphant as I am?

STANLEY   The Lords at Pomfret, when they rode from London,

Were jocund and supposed their states were sure,
And they indeed had no cause to mistrust;
But yet you see how soon the day o'ercast.
This sudden stab of rancour I misdoubt:[107]
Pray God, I say, I prove a needless coward!
What, shall we toward the Tower? The day is spent.[108]

HASTINGS Come, come; have with you. Wot you what, my Lord?
Today the Lords you talked of are beheaded.

STANLEY They, for their truth, might better wear their heads   90
Than some that have accused them wear their hats.
But come, my Lord, let's away.

                        Enter a PURSUIVANT.[109]

HASTINGS Go on before; I'll talk with this good fellow.
                                    [*Exeunt Stanley and Catesby.*
            – How now, sirrah? How goes the world with thee?

PURSUIV. The better that your Lordship please to ask.

HASTINGS I tell thee, man, 'tis better with me now
Than when thou met'st me last where now we meet:
Then was I going prisoner to the Tower,
By the suggestion of the Queen's allies;
But now, I tell thee (keep it to thyself)   100
This day those enemies are put to death,
And I in better state than e'er I was.

PURSUIV. God hold it, to your Honour's good content!

HASTINGS Gramercy, fellow: there, drink that for me.
                            [*Hastings throws a purse to him.*

PURSUIV. I thank your Honour.   [*Exit.*

                        Enter a PRIEST (*Sir John*).

PRIEST Well met, my Lord; I am glad to see your Honour.

HASTINGS I thank thee, good Sir John, with all my heart.
I am in your debt for your last exercise:
Come the next Sabbath, and I will content you.   110
                            [*He whispers in his ear.*

                        Enter BUCKINGHAM.

PRIEST I'll wait upon your Lordship.   [*Exit.*

BUCKING. What, talking with a priest, Lord Chamberlain?
Your friends at Pomfret, they do need the priest;

Your Honour hath no shriving work in hand.

HASTINGS Good faith, and when I met this holy man,
The men you talk of came into my mind.
What, go you toward the Tower?

BUCKING. I do, my Lord; but long I cannot stay there.
I shall return before your Lordship thence.

HASTINGS Nay, like enough, for I stay dinner there.   120

BUCKING. [*aside:*] And supper too, although thou know'st it not.
[*Aloud:*] Come, will you go?

HASTINGS   I'll wait upon your Lordship.
[*Exeunt.*

SCENE 3.

Yorkshire. Pontefract ('Pomfret') Castle.

Enter RATCLIFFE, *with* HALBERDIERS, *conducting the*
noblemen RIVERS, GREY *and* VAUGHAN *to death.*[110]

RIVERS   Sir Richard Ratcliffe, let me tell thee this:
Today shalt thou behold a subject die
For truth, for duty, and for loyalty.

GREY   [*to Rat.:*] God bless the Prince from all the pack of you!
A knot you are of damnèd blood-suckers.

VAUGHAN   [*to Rat.:*] You live that shall cry woe for this hereafter.

RATCLIFFE Dispatch; the limit of your lives is out.

RIVERS   – O Pomfret, Pomfret! O thou bloody prison,
Fatal and ominous to noble peers!
Within the guilty closure of thy walls   10
Richard the Second here was hacked to death;
And, for more slander to thy dismal seat,[111]
We give to thee our guiltless blood to drink.

GREY   Now Margaret's curse is fall'n upon our heads,
When she exclaimed on Hastings, you, and I,
For standing by when Richard stabbed her son.

RIVERS   Then cursed she Richard, then cursed she Buckingham,
Then cursed she Hastings.[112] – O remember, God,
To hear her prayer for them, as now for us.
And for my sister and her princely sons,   20
Be satisfied, dear God, with our true blood,

Which, as Thou know'st, unjustly must be spilt.

RATCLIFFE Make haste: the hour of death is expiate.

RIVERS   – Come, Grey, come, Vaughan: let us here embrace.
            Farewell, until we meet again in Heaven.
                    [*Rivers, Grey and Vaughan embrace. Exeunt all.*

SCENE 4.

A room in the Tower of London.

Enter BUCKINGHAM, STANLEY, HASTINGS, *the* BISHOP OF ELY,
LORD LOVEL, CATESBY *and* OTHERS. *They sit at a table.*[113]

HASTINGS Now, noble peers, the cause why we are met
          Is to determine of the coronation.
          In God's name, speak: when is the royal day?

BUCKING. Is all things ready for the royal time?

STANLEY   It is, and wants but nomination.

ELY   Tomorrow, then, I judge a happy day.

BUCKING. Who knows the Lord Protector's mind herein?
          Who is most inward with the noble Duke?

ELY   Your Grace, we think, should soonest know his mind.

BUCKING. We know each other's faces; for our hearts,   10
          He knows no more of mine than I of yours;
          Or I of his, my Lord, than you of mine.
          – Lord Hastings, you and he are near in love.

HASTINGS I thank his Grace; I know he loves me well;
          But, for his purpose in the coronation,
          I have not sounded him, nor he delivered
          His gracious pleasure any way therein.
          – But you, my honourable Lords, may name the time;
          And in the Duke's behalf I'll give my voice,
          Which, I presume, he'll take in gentle part.   20

                    Enter RICHARD.

ELY   In happy time, here comes the Duke himself.

RICHARD   My noble Lords and cousins all, good morrow.
          I have been long a sleeper; but I trust
          My absence doth neglect no great design
          Which by my presence might have been concluded.

BUCKING.   Had you not come upon your cue, my Lord,
             William Lord Hastings had pronounced your part,
             I mean your voice, for crowning of the King.

RICHARD   Than my Lord Hastings no man might be bolder:
             His Lordship knows me well, and loves me well.   30
             – My lord of Ely, when I was last in Holborn,
             I saw good strawberries in your garden there:[114]
             I do beseech you, send for some of them.

ELY   Marry, and will, my Lord, with all my heart.   [*Exit.*

RICHARD   Cousin of Buckingham, a word with you.

             Richard addresses Buckingham privately:

             Catesby hath sounded Hastings in our business,
             And finds the testy gentleman so hot
             That he will lose his head ere give consent
             His master's child, as worshipfully he terms it,
             Shall lose the royalty of England's throne.   40

BUCKING.   Withdraw yourself a while: I'll go with you.
                         [*Exeunt Richard and Buckingham.*

STANLEY   We have not yet set down this day of triumph.
             Tomorrow, in my judgement, is too sudden;
             For I myself am not so well provided
             As else I would be, were the day prolonged.

             Enter the BISHOP OF ELY.

ELY   Where is my Lord the Duke of Gloucester?
             I have sent for these strawberries.

HASTINGS   His Grace looks cheerfully and smooth this morning:
             There's some conceit or other likes him well,
             When that he bids good-morrow with such spirit.   50
             I think there's ne'er a man in Christendom
             Can lesser hide his love or hate than he,
             For by his face straight shall you know his heart.

STANLEY   What of his heart perceive you in his face
             By any livelihood[115] he showed today?

HASTINGS   Marry, that with no man here he is offended;
             For, were he, he had shown it in his looks.

             Enter RICHARD *and* BUCKINGHAM.

RICHARD   I pray you all, tell me what they deserve
             That do conspire my death with div'lish plots

| | Of damnèd witchcraft, and that have prevailed | 60 |
| | Upon my body with their hellish charms? | |

HASTINGS   The tender love I bear your Grace, my Lord,
            Makes me most forward in this princely presence
            To doom th'offenders, whosoe'er they be:
            I say, my Lord, they have deservèd death.
RICHARD   Then be your eyes the witness of their evil.

                                    [*He bares his left arm.*

            Look how I am bewitched: behold, mine arm
            Is like a blasted sapling withered up:
            And this is Edward's wife, that monstrous witch,
            Consorted with that harlot, strumpet Shore,   70
            That by their witchcraft thus have markèd me.[116]
HASTINGS   If they have done this deed, my noble Lord –
RICHARD   'If'! Thou protector of this damnèd strumpet,
            Talk'st thou to me of 'ifs'? Thou art a traitor. –
            Off with his head! Now, by Saint Paul I swear,
            I will not dine until I see the same.
            Lovel and Catesby, look that it be done;
            The rest that love me, rise and follow me.

                        [*Exeunt all but Hastings, Catesby and Lovel.*

HASTINGS   Woe, woe for England; not a whit for me;
            For I, too fond, might have prevented this.   80
            Stanley did dream the boar did raze our helms,
            And I did scorn it, and disdain to fly;
            Three times today my footcloth horse did stumble,
            And started when he looked upon the Tower,
            As loath to bear me to the slaughter-house.
            O, now I need the priest that spake to me!
            I now repent I told the pursuivant,
            As too triumphing, how mine enemies
            Today at Pomfret bloodily were butchered,
            And I myself secure in grace and favour.   90
            – O Margaret, Margaret, now thy heavy curse
            Is lighted on poor Hastings' wretched head!
CATESBY   Come, come, dispatch: the Duke would be at dinner.
            Make a short shrift: he longs to see your head.
HASTINGS   O momentary grace of mortal men,
            Which we more hunt for than the grace of God!

Who builds his hope in air of your good looks
Lives like a drunken sailor on a mast,
Ready with every nod to tumble down
Into the fatal bowels of the deep.   100
CATESBY   Come, come, dispatch: 'tis bootless to exclaim.
HASTINGS   O bloody Richard! Miserable England,
I prophesy the fearfull'st time to thee
That ever wretched age hath looked upon.[117]
– Come, lead me to the block; bear him my head.
They smile at me who shortly shall be dead.   [*Exeunt.*

SCENE 5.

London. A gateway in the wall of the Tower.

Enter, from within, RICHARD *and* BUCKINGHAM,
in remarkably-dilapidated rusty armour.[118]

RICHARD   Come, cousin, canst thou quake, and change thy colour,
Murther thy breath in middle of a word,
And then again begin, and stop again,
As if thou wert distraught and mad with terror?
BUCKING.   Tut, I can counterfeit the deep tragedian,
Speak and look back, and pry on every side,
Tremble and start at wagging of a straw,
Intending deep suspicion. Ghastly looks
Are at my service, like enforcèd smiles;
And both are ready in their offices,   10
At any time, to grace my stratagems.[119]
RICHARD   Here comes the Mayor.

Enter the MAYOR.

BUCKING.   Let me alone to entertain him. – Lord Mayor –
RICHARD   [*as if to someone within:*] Look to the drawbridge there!
BUCKING.   Hark! A drum!
RICHARD   [*as if to someone within:*] Catesby, o'erlook the walls!
BUCKING.   Lord Mayor, the reason we have sent –
RICHARD   [*to Mayor:*] Look back, defend thee, here are enemies!
BUCKING.   God and our innocence defend and guard us!
RICHARD   O, O, be quiet! It is Catesby.   20

Enter CATESBY *with* HASTINGS' *head.*

CATESBY   Here is the head of that ignoble traitor,
The dangerous and unsuspected Hastings.

RICHARD   So dear I loved the man, that I must weep.
I took him for the plainest harmless creature
That breathed upon the earth a Christian;
Made him my book, wherein my soul recorded
The history of all her secret thoughts.
So smooth he daubed his vice with show of virtue
That, his apparent open guilt omitted –
I mean his conversation with Shore's wife –   30
He lived from all attainder of suspécts.

BUCKING.   Well, well, he was the covert'st sheltered traitor.
[*To Mayor:*] Would you imagine, or almóst believe,
Were't not that by great preservatión
We live to tell it, that the subtle traitor
This day had plotted, in the Council-house,
To murther me and my good Lord of Gloucester?

MAYOR   Had he done so?

RICHARD   What! Think you we are Turks or infidels,
Or that we would, against the form of law,   40
Proceed thus rashly in the villain's death,
But that the éxtreme peril of the case,
The peace of England and our persons' safety,
Enforced us to this executión?

MAYOR   Now, fair befall you! He deserved his death;
And your good Graces both have well proceeded,
To warn false traitors from the like attempts.
I never looked for better at his hands,
After he once fell in with Mistress Shore.

RICHARD   Yet had we not determined he should die,   50
Until your Lordship came to see his end,
Which now the loving haste of these our friends,
Something against our meanings, have prevented:
Because, my Lord, I would have had you hear
The traitor speak and tim'rously confess
The manner and the purpose of his treasons;
That you might well have signified the same
Unto the citizens, who haply may

Miscónster us in him, and wail his death.[120]

MAYOR But, my good Lord, your Grace's words shall serve 60
As well as I had seen and heard him speak:
And do not doubt, right noble Princes both,
But I'll acquaint our duteous citizens
With all your just proceedings in this cause.

RICHARD And to that end we wished your Lordship here,
T'avoid the censures of the carping world.

BUCKING. Which since you come too late of our intent,
Yet witness what you hear we did intend;
And so, my good Lord Mayor, we bid farewell.

                                        [*Exit Mayor.*

RICHARD Go, after, after, cousin Buckingham! 70
The Mayor towards Guildhall[121] hies him in all post.
There, at your meet'st advantage of the time,
Infer the bastardy of Edward's children.
Tell them how Edward put to death a citizen,
Only for saying he would make his son
Heir to the Crown, meaning indeed his house,
Which, by the sign thereof, was termèd so.[122]
Moreover, urge his hateful luxury
And bestial appetite in change of lust,
Which stretched unto their servants, daughters, wives, 80
Even where his raging eye or savage heart
Without control listed to make a prey.
Nay, for a need, thus far come near my person:
Tell them, when that my mother went with child
Of that insatiate Edward, noble York,
My princely father, then had wars in France;
And, by true computation of the time,
Found that the issue was not his begot;
Which well appeared in his lineaments,
Being nothing like the noble Duke my father: 90
Yet touch this sparingly, as 'twere far off,
Because, my Lord, you know my mother lives.

BUCKING. Doubt not, my Lord, I'll play the orator
As if the golden fee for which I plead
Were for myself; and so, my Lord, adieu.

RICHARD If you thrive well, bring them to Baynard's Castle,

Where you shall find me well accompanied
With reverend fathers and well-learnèd bishops.
BUCKING. I go, and towards three or four o'clock
Look for the news that the Guildhall affords.   [Exit. 100
RICHARD Now will I go to take some privy order[123]
To draw the brats of Clarence out of sight;
And to give notice that no manner person
Have any time recourse unto the Princes.   [Exeunt.

SCENE 6.

London. A street.

Enter a SCRIVENER with a paper in his hand.

SCRIVENER Here is the indictment of the good Lord Hastings,
Which in a set hand fairly is engrossed,
That it may be today read o'er in Paul's.
And mark how well the sequel hangs together:
Eleven hours I have spent to write it over,
For yesternight by Catesby was it sent me;
The precedent was full as long a-doing;
And yet, within these five hours, Hastings lived,
Untainted, unexamined, free, at liberty.
Here's a good world the while! Who is so gross,   10
That cannot see this palpable device?[124]
Yet who's so bold, but says he sees it not?
Bad is the world; and all will come to nought,
When such ill dealing must be seen in thought.[125] [Exit.

SCENE 7.

London. A courtyard before Baynard's Castle.

Enter RICHARD *and* BUCKINGHAM *from separate doors, meeting.*

RICHARD   How now, how now: what say the citizens?
BUCKING.   Now, by the holy Mother of our Lord,
             The citizens are mum, say not a word.
RICHARD   Touched you the bastardy of Edward's children?
BUCKING.   I did; with his contráct with Lady Lucy,
             And his contráct by deputy in France;[126]
             Th'insatiate greediness of his desire,
             And his enforcement of the city wives;
             His tyranny for trifles;[127] his own bastardy,
             As being got, your father then in France,   10
             And his resemblance, being not like the Duke:
             Withal I did infer your lineaments,
             Being the right idea of your father,
             Both in your form and nobleness of mind;
             Laid open all your victories in Scotland,[128]
             Your discipline in war, wisdom in peace,
             Your bounty, virtue, fair humility;
             Indeed, left nothing fitting for your purpose
             Untouched or slightly handled in discourse;
             And when mine oratory drew toward end,   20
             I bid them that did love their country's good
             Cry 'God save Richard, England's royal King!'.
RICHARD   And did they so?
BUCKING.   No, so God help me, they spake not a word;
             But, like dumb statuas[129] or breathing stones,
             Stared each on other and looked deadly pale.
             Which when I saw, I reprehended them,
             And asked the Mayor what meant this wilful silence.
             His answer was, the people were not used
             To be spoke to but by the Récorder.[130]   30
             Then he was urged to tell my tale again:
             'Thus saith the Duke, thus hath the Duke inferred';
             But nothing spoke in warrant from himself.
             When he had done, some followers of mine own,

At lower end of the hall, hurled up their caps,
And some ten voices cried 'God save King Richard!';
And thus I took the vantage of those few:
'Thanks, gentle citizens and friends,' quoth I,
'This general applause and cheerful shout
Argues your wisdoms and your love to Richard';   40
And even here brake off and came away.

RICHARD   What tongueless blocks were they! Would they
                                            not speak?

BUCKING.   No, by my troth, my Lord.

RICHARD   Will not the Mayor then and his brethren come?

BUCKING.   The Mayor is here at hand: intend some fear;
Be not you spoke with, but by mighty suit;
And look you get a prayer-book in your hand,
And stand between two churchmen, good my Lord:
For on that ground I'll make a holy descant.
And be not easily won to our requests: 50
Play the maid's part: still answer 'Nay', and take it.

RICHARD   I go; and if you plead as well for them
As I can say 'Nay' to thee for myself,
No doubt we bring it to a happy issue.

                                            [Knocking.

BUCKING.   Go, go up to the leads; the Lord Mayor knocks.

                                            [Exit Richard.

          Enter the MAYOR, ALDERMEN and CITIZENS.

– Welcome, my Lord: I dance attendance here;
I think the Duke will not be spoke withal.

              Enter CATESBY above.

– Catesby, what says your Lord to my request?

CATESBY   He doth entreat your Grace, my noble Lord,
To visit him tomorrow or next day.   60
He is within, with two right reverend fathers,
Divinely bent to meditatiòn;
And in no worldly suits would he be moved,
To draw him from his holy exercise.

BUCKING.   Return, good Catesby, to the gracious Duke:
Tell him, myself, the Mayor, and aldermen,
In deep designs, in matter of great moment,

No less importing than our general good,
Are come to have some conference with his Grace.

CATESBY   I'll signify so much unto him straight.   [*Exit.* 70

BUCKING.   [*to Mayor:*] Ah ha, my Lord, this Prince is not an Edward!
He is not lolling on a lewd love-bed,
But on his knees at meditatiòn;
Not dallying with a brace of courtesans,
But meditating with two deep divines;
Not sleeping, to engross his idle body,
But praying, to enrich his watchful soul.
Happy were England, would this virtuous Prince
Take on his grace the sovereignty thereof;
But, sure, I fear, we shall not win him to it.   80

MAYOR   Marry, God defend his Grace should say us 'nay'!

BUCKING.   I fear he will. Here Catesby comes again.

Enter CATESBY *above.*

– Now, Catesby, what says his Grace?

CATESBY   He wonders to what end you have assembled
Such troops of citizens to come to him,
His Grace not being warned thereof before:
He fears, my Lord, you mean no good to him.

BUCKING.   Sorry I am my noble cousin should
Suspect me that I mean no good to him:
By Heaven, we come to him in perfit love;   90
And so once more return and tell his Grace.

[*Exit Catesby.*

– When holy and devout religious men
Are at their beads, 'tis much to draw them thence,
So sweet is zealous contemplation.

Enter RICHARD *aloft, between* TWO BISHOPS. *Enter* CATESBY *below.*

MAYOR   See, where his Grace stands, 'tween two clergymen!

BUCKING.   Two props of virtue for a Christian prince,
To stay him from the fall of vanity;
And, see, a book of prayer in his hand:
True ornaments to know a holy man.
[*To Richard:*] Famous Plantagenet, most gracious Prince,   100
Lend favourable ear to our requests;
And pardon us the interruptiòn

	Of thy devotion and right Christian zeal.
RICHARD	My Lord, there needs no such apology.
	I do beseech your Grace to pardon me,
	Who, earnest in the service of my God,
	Deferred the visitation of my friends.
	But, leaving this, what is your Grace's pleasure?
BUCKING.	Even that (I hope) which pleaseth God above
	And all good men of this ungoverned isle.

RICHARD   I do suspect I have done some offence
            That seems disgracious in the city's eye,
            And that you come to reprehend my ignorance.
BUCKING.   You have, my Lord: would it might please your Grace,
            On our entreaties, to amend your fault!
RICHARD   Else wherefore breathe I in a Christian land?
BUCKING.   Know, then, it is your fault that you resign
            The súpreme seat, the throne majestical,
            The sceptred office of your ancestors,
            Your state of fortune and your due of birth,
            The lineal glory of your royal House,
            To the corruption of a blemished stock;
            Whiles, in the mildness of your sleepy thoughts,
            Which here we waken to our country's good,
            The noble isle doth want her proper limbs;
            Her face defaced with scars of infamy,
            Her royal stock graft with ignoble plants
            And almost shouldered in the swallowing gulf
            Of dark forgetfulness and deep oblivion.
            Which to recure, we heartily solicit
            Your gracious self to take on you the charge
            And kingly government of this your land;
            Not as Protector, steward, substitute,
            Or lowly factor for another's gain,
            But as successively, from blood to blood,
            Your right of birth, your empery, your own.
            For this, consorted with the citizens,
            Your very worshipful and loving friends,
            And by their ve'ment instigatiòn,[131]
            In this just cause come I to move your Grace.
RICHARD   I cannot tell if to depart in silence

110

120

130

140

Or bitterly to speak in your reproof
Best fitteth my degree or your condition.
If not to answer, you might haply think
Tongue-tied ambition, not replying, yielded
To bear the golden yoke of sovereignty,
Which fondly you would here impose on me;
If to reprove you for this suit of yours,
So seasoned with your faithful love to me,
Then, on the other side, I checked my friends.   150
Therefore, to speak, and to avoid the first,
And then, in speaking, not to incur the last,
Definitively thus I answer you:[132]
Your love deserves my thanks, but my desert
Unmeritable shuns your high request.
First, if all obstacles were cut away
And that my path were even to the crown,
As the ripe revenue and due of birth,
Yet so much is my poverty of spirit,
So mighty and so many my defécts,   160
That I would rather hide me from my greatness,
Being a bark to brook no mighty sea,
Than in my greatness covet to be hid
And in the vapour of my glory smothered.
But, God be thanked, there is no need of me,
And much I need, to help you, were there need:
The royal tree hath left us royal fruit,
Which, mellowed by the stealing hours of time,
Will well become the seat of majesty,
And make (no doubt) us happy by his reign.   170
On him I lay that you would lay on me,
The right and fortune of his happy stars,
Which God defend that I should wring from him!
BUCKING. My Lord, this argues conscience in your Grace;
But the respects thereof are nice and trivial,
All circumstances well consideréd.
You say that Edward is your brother's son:
So say we too, but not by Edward's wife;
For first was he contráct to Lady Lucy[133] –
Your mother lives a witness to his vow –   180

And afterward by substitute betrothed
To Bona, sister to the King of France.
These both put off, a poor petitioner,[134]
A care-crazed mother to a many sons,
A beauty-waning and distressèd widow,
Even in the afternoon of her best days,
Made prize and purchase of his wanton eye,
Seduced the pitch and height of his degree
To base declension and loathed bigamy.
By her, in his unlawful bed, he got   190
This Edward, whom our manners call 'the Prince'.[135]
More bitterly could I expostulate,
Save that, for reverence to some alive,
I give a sparing limit to my tongue.
Then, good my Lord, take to your royal self
This proffered benefit of dignity;
If not to bless us and the land withal,
Yet to draw forth your noble ancestry
From the corruption of abusing times
Unto a lineal true-derivèd course.   200

MAYOR   Do, good my Lord, your citizens entreat you.
BUCKING.   Refuse not, mighty Lord, this proffered love.
CATESBY   O, make them joyful: grant their lawful suit!
RICHARD   Alas, why would you heap this care on me?
          I am unfit for state and majesty.
          I do beseech you, take it not amiss:
          I cannot nor I will not yield to you.
BUCKING.   If you refuse it, as, in love and zeal,
          Loath to depose the child, your brother's son;
          As well we know your tenderness of heart   210
          And gentle, kind, effeminate remorse,
          Which we have noted in you to your kindred,
          And egally indeed to all estates:
          Yet know, whe'er you accept our suit or no,
          Your brother's son shall never reign our King,
          But we will plant some other in the throne
          To the disgrace and downfall of your House;
          And in this resolution here we leave you.
          – Come, citizens. Zounds! I'll entreat no more.

RICHARD   O, do not swear, my Lord of Buckingham!   220
                   [*Exeunt Buckingham, Mayor, aldermen and citizens.*
CATESBY   Call him again, sweet Prince: accept their suit.
                   If you deny them, all the land will rue it.
RICHARD   Will you enforce me to a world of cares?
                   Call them again: I am not made of stone,
                   But penetrable to your kind entreaties,
                   Albeit against my conscience and my soul.

                   Catesby calls them. Soon enter, below, BUCKINGHAM,
                                   MAYOR, ALDERMEN *and* CITIZENS.

                   Cousin of Buckingham, and sage grave men,
                   Since you will buckle Fortune on my back,
                   To bear her burthen, whe'er I will or no,
                   I must have patience to endure the load.   230
                   But if black scandal or foul-faced reproach
                   Attend the sequel of your imposition,
                   Your mere enforcement shall acquittance me
                   From all the ímpure blots and stains thereof;
                   For God doth know, and you may partly see,
                   How far I am from the desire of this.
MAYOR   God bless your Grace! We see it, and will say it.
RICHARD   In saying so, you shall but say the truth.
BUCKING.   Then I salute you with this royal title:
                   Long live King Richard, England's worthy King!   240
ALL   [*except Richard:*] Amen.
BUCKING.   Tomorrow may it please you to be crowned?
RICHARD   Even when you please, for you will have it so.
BUCKING.   Tomorrow, then, we will attend your Grace:
                   And so most joyfully we take our leave.
RICHARD   [*to Bishops:*] Come, let us to our holy work again.
                   – Farewell, my cousin; farewell, gentle friends.
                                                                   [*Exeunt.*

ACT 4, SCENE 1.

London. Before the Tower.

Enter, from one door, QUEEN ELIZABETH, *the* DUCHESS OF YORK
and the MARQUIS OF DORSET; *meeting, from another door,*
ANNE, DUCHESS OF GLOUCESTER, *and*
LADY MARGARET PLANTAGENET, *Clarence's young daughter.*

DUCHESS Who meets us here? My niece Plantagenet,
Led in the hand of her kind aunt of Gloucester?[136]
Now, for my life, she's wand'ring to the Tower,
On pure heart's love, to greet the tender Princes.
– Daughter, well met.

ANNE   God give your Graces both
A happy and a joyful time of day!

Q. ELIZAB. As much to you, good sister! Whither away?[137]

ANNE No farther than the Tower, and, as I guess,
Upon the like devotion as yourselves,
To gratulate the gentle Princes there.   10

Q. ELIZAB. Kind sister, thanks: we'll enter all together.

Enter, from the Tower, Lieutenant BRAKENBURY.

And, in good time, here the Lieutenant comes.
– Master Lieutenant, pray you, by your leave,
How doth the Prince, and my young son of York?

BRAKEN. Right well, dear madam. By your patiènce,
I may not suffer you to visit them:
The King hath strictly charged the contrary.

Q. ELIZAB. The King! Who's that?

BRAKEN.   I mean, the Lord Protector.

Q. ELIZAB. The Lord protect him from that kingly title!
Hath he set bounds between their love and me?   20
I am their mother: who shall bar me from them?

DUCHESS I am their father's mother: I will see them.

ANNE Their aunt I am in law, in love their mother;
Then bring me to their sights: I'll bear thy blame,
And take thy office from thee, on my peril.

BRAKEN. No, madam, no; I may not leave it so:

I am bound by oath, and therefore pardon me.

[*Exit.*

Enter STANLEY.

STANLEY   Let me but meet you, ladies, one hour hence,
             And I'll salute your Grace of York as mother
             And reverend looker-on of two fair Queens.[138]   30
             [*To Anne:*] Come, madam, you must straight to
                                              Westminster,
             There to be crownèd Richard's royal Queen.

Q. ELIZAB.   Ah, cut my lace asunder,
             That my pent heart may have some scope to beat,
             Or else I swoon with this dead-killing news!

ANNE   Despiteful tidings! O unpleasing news!

DORSET   Be of good cheer. – Mother, how fares your Grace?

Q. ELIZAB.   O Dorset, speak not to me, get thee gone!
             Death and destruction dogs thee at thy heels;
             Thy mother's name is ominous to children.   40
             If thou wilt outstrip death, go cross the seas,
             And live with Richmond, from the reach of Hell:[139]
             Go, hie thee, hie thee from this slaughter-house,
             Lest thou increase the number of the dead,
             And make me die the thrall of Margaret's curse,
             Nor mother, wife, nor England's counted Queen.

STANLEY   Full of wise care is this your counsel, madam.
             [*To Dorset:*] Take all the swift advantage of the hours.
             You shall have letters from me to my son[140]
             In your behalf, to meet you on the way: 50
             Be not tane tardy by unwise delay.

DUCHESS   O ill-dispersing wind of misery!
             O my accursèd womb, the bed of death!
             A cockatrice hast thou hatched to the world,
             Whose unavoided eye is murtherous.

STANLEY   Come, madam, come; I in all haste was sent.

ANNE   And I with all unwillingness will go.
             O, would to God that the inclusive verge
             Of golden metal that must round my brow
             Were red-hot steel, to sear me to the brains!   60
             Anointed let me be with deadly venom,

And die ere men can say 'God save the Queen!'.

Q. ELIZAB. Go, go, poor soul; I envy not thy glory.
To feed my humour, wish thyself no harm.

ANNE   No? Why, when he that is my husband now
Came to me, as I followed Henry's corse,
When scarce the blood was well washed from his hands
Which issued from my other angel husband,
And that dear saint which then I weeping followed –
O, when, I say, I looked on Richard's face,   70
This was my wish: 'Be thou', quoth I, 'accursed,
For making me, so young, so old a widow!
And, when thou wed'st, let sorrow haunt thy bed;
And be thy wife, if any be so mad,
More miserable by the life of thee
Than thou hast made me by my dear Lord's death!'.
Lo, ere I can repeat this curse again,
Within so small a time, my woman's heart
Grossly grew captive to his honey words,
And proved the subject of mine own soul's curse,   80
Which hitherto hath held mine eyes from rest;
For never yet one hour in his bed
Did I enjoy the golden dew of sleep,
But with his timorous dreams was still awaked.
Besides, he hates me for my father Warwick;
And will, no doubt, shortly be rid of me.

Q. ELIZAB. Poor heart, adieu! I pity thy complaining.

ANNE   No more than with my soul I mourn for yours.

Q. ELIZAB. Farewell, thou woeful welcomer of glory!

ANNE   Adieu, poor soul, that tak'st thy leave of it!   90

DUCHESS [to Dorset:] Go thou to Richmond, and good fortune
                                                guide thee!
[To Anne:] Go thou to Richard, and good angels
                                                tend thee!
[To Queen Elizabeth:] Go thou to sanctuary, and
                                    good thoughts possess thee!
– I to my grave, where peace and rest lie with me!
Eighty odd years of sorrow have I seen,
And each hour's joy wracked with a week of teen.

Q. ELIZAB. Stay, yet look back with me unto the Tower.

– Pity, you ancient stones, those tender babes
Whom envy hath immured within your walls:
Rough cradle for such little pretty ones!   100
Rude raggèd nurse, old sullen playfellow
For tender princes, use my babies well!
So foolish sorrow bids your stones farewell.[141] [*Exeunt.*]

SCENE 2.

London. The throne-room at the Palace.

Sennet. Enter RICHARD *in pomp, crowned,*
BUCKINGHAM, CATESBY, NOBLEMEN *and a* PAGE.

K.RICHARD Stand all apart. – Cousin of Buckingham!
BUCKING. My gracious sovereign!
K.RICHARD Give me thy hand.   [*Sennet. He ascends the throne.*]
                              Thus high, by thy advice,
And thy assistance, is King Richard seated:
                    [*Richard converses privately with Buckingham:*]
But shall we wear these glories for a day?
Or shall they last, and we rejoice in them?
BUCKING. Still live they, and for ever let them last!
K.RICHARD Ah Buckingham, now do I play the touch,[142]
To try if thou be current gold indeed:
Young Edward lives; think now what I would speak.   10
BUCKING. Say on, my loving Lord.
K.RICHARD Why, Buckingham, I say I would be King.
BUCKING. Why, so you are, my thrice-renownèd Lord.
K.RICHARD Ha? Am I King? 'Tis so – but Edward lives.
BUCKING. True, noble Prince.
K.RICHARD   O bitter consequence!
That Edward still should live, 'true, noble Prince'!
Cousin, thou wast not wont to be so dull.
Shall I be plain? I wish the bastards dead,
And I would have it suddenly performed.
What say'st thou now? Speak suddenly: be brief.   20
BUCKING. Your Grace may do your pleasure.
K.RICHARD Tut, tut, thou art all ice; thy kindness freezes:
Say, have I thy consent that they shall die?

BUCKING. Give me some little breath, some pause, dear Lord,
          Before I positively speak in this:
          I will resolve you herein presently.   [*Exit.*

CATESBY   [*to bystander:*] The King is angry: see, he gnaws his lip.

K.RICHARD [*aside:*] I will converse with iron-witted fools
          And unrespective boys: none are for me
                              [*He descends from the throne.*
          That look into me with considerate eyes: 30
          High-reaching Buckingham grows circumspect.
          – Boy!

PAGE   My Lord?
                        [*Richard converses privately with him:*

K.RICHARD Know'st thou not any whom corrupting gold
          Will tempt unto a close exploit of death?

PAGE   I know a discontented gentleman
          Whose humble means match not his haughty spirit:
          Gold were as good as twenty orators,
          And will, no doubt, tempt him to anything.

K.RICHARD What is his name?

PAGE   His name, my Lord, is Tyrrel.   40

K.RICHARD I partly know the man: go, call him hither, boy.
                                            [*Exit page.*

          [*Aside:*] The deep-revolving witty Buckingham
          No more shall be the neighbour to my counsels.
          Hath he so long held out with me untired,
          And stops he now for breath? Well, be it so.

                    Enter STANLEY.

          – How now, Lord Stanley: what's the news?

STANLEY   Know, my loving Lord,
          The Marquis Dorset, as I hear, is fled
          To Richmond in the parts where he abides.
                                      [*He stands apart.*

K.RICHARD – Come hither, Catesby. Rumour it abroad   50
          That Anne, my wife, is very grievous sick:
          I will take order for her keeping close.[143]
          Inquire me out some mean poor gentleman,
          Whom I will marry straight to Clarence' daughter.
          The boy is foolish, and I fear not him.[144]

Look how thou dream'st! I say again, give out
That Anne, my Queen, is sick and like to die.
About it, for it stands me much upon
To stop all hopes whose growth may damage me.

[Exit Catesby.

I must be married to my brother's daughter,[145]   60
Or else my kingdom stands on brittle glass.
Murther her brothers, and then marry her?
Uncertain way of gain! But I am in
So far in blood that sin will pluck on sin.
Tear-falling pity dwells not in this eye.

Enter Sir James TYRREL.

    – Is thy name Tyrrel?

TYRREL   James Tyrrel, and your most obedient subject.

K.RICHARD Art thou indeed?

TYRREL   Prove me, my gracious Lord.

[Richard takes him aside:

K.RICHARD Dar'st thou resolve to kill a friend of mine?

TYRREL   Please you, I had rather kill two enemies.   70

K.RICHARD Why, there thou hast it: two deep enemies,
Foes to my rest, and my sweet sleep's disturbers,
Are they that I would have thee deal upon:
Tyrrel, I mean those bastards in the Tower.

TYRREL   Let me have open means to come to them,
And soon I'll rid you from the fear of them.

K.RICHARD Thou sing'st sweet music. Hark, come hither, Tyrrel:

[Tyrrel approaches and kneels.

Go, by this token; rise, and lend thine ear.

[He gives the token to Tyrrel. Tyrrel rises.
Richard whispers instructions.

[*Aloud:*] There is no more but so: say it is done,
And I will love thee, and prefer thee for it.   80

TYRREL   I will dispatch it straight.   [*Exit.*

Enter BUCKINGHAM.

BUCKING. My Lord, I have considered in my mind
The late request that you did sound me in.

K.RICHARD Well, let that rest. Dorset is fled to Richmond.

BUCKING. I hear the news, my Lord.

K.RICHARD Stanley, he is your wife's son:[146] well look to it.

BUCKING. My Lord, I claim the gift, my due by promise,
For which your honour and your faith is pawned:
Th'Earldom of Her'ford and the movables
Which you have promisèd I shall possess.   90

K.RICHARD Stanley, look to your wife: if she convey
Letters to Richmond, you shall answer it.

BUCKING. What says your Highness to my just request?

K.RICHARD I do remember me, Henry the Sixth
Did prophesy that Richmond should be King,
When Richmond was a little peevish boy.[147]
A king! Perhaps, perhaps . . .

BUCKING.   My Lord!

K.RICHARD How chance the prophet could not at that time
Have told me, I being by, that I should kill him?

BUCKING. My Lord, your promise for the Earldom –   100

K.RICHARD Richmond! When last I was at Exeter,
The Mayor in courtesy showed me the castle,
And called it Rougemont: at which name I started,
Because a bard of Ireland told me once
I should not live long after I saw Richmond.[148]

BUCKING. My Lord!

K.RICHARD   Ay, what's o'clock?

BUCKING. I am thus bold to put your Grace in mind
Of what you promised me.

K.RICHARD   Well, but what's o'clock?

BUCKING. Upon the stroke of ten.

K.RICHARD   Well, let it strike.

BUCKING. Why let it strike?   110

K.RICHARD Because that, like a Jack, thou keep'st the stroke
Betwixt thy begging and my meditation.
I am not in the giving vein today.[149]

BUCKING. May it please you to resolve me in my suit?

K.RICHARD Thou troublest me; I am not in the vein.

                                    [Exit, followed by all but Buckingham.

BUCKING. And is it thus? Repays he my deep service
With such contempt? Made I him King for this?
O, let me think on Hastings, and be gone
To Brecknock,[150] while my fearful head is on!   [Exit.

SCENE 3.

London. The Palace.

Enter TYRREL.

TYRREL   The tyrannous and bloody act is done,
The most arch deed of piteous massacre
That ever yet this land was guilty of.
Dighton and Forrest, who I did suborn
To do this piece of ruthless butchery,
Albeit they were fleshed villains, bloody dogs,
Melted with tenderness and mild compassion,
Wept like two children in their deaths' sad story.
'O, thus', quoth Dighton, 'lay the gentle babes';
'Thus, thus', quoth Forrest, 'girdling one another   10
Within their alabaster innocent arms;
Their lips were four red roses on a stalk,
Which in their summer beauty kissed each other.
A book of prayers on their pillow lay;
Which once', quoth Forrest, 'almost changed my mind;
But O, the Divel' – There the villain stopped,
Whilst Dighton thus told on: 'We smotherèd
The most replenishèd sweet work of Nature
That from the prime creation e'er she framed.'
Hence both are gone with conscience and remorse;   20
They could not speak; and so I left them both,
To bear this tidings to the bloody King.
And here he comes.

Enter KING RICHARD.

                                    – All health, my sovereign Lord!
K.RICHARD   Kind Tyrrel, am I happy in thy news?
TYRREL   If to have done the thing you gave in charge
Beget your happiness, be happy then,
For it is done.
K.RICHARD   But didst thou see them dead?
TYRREL   I did, my Lord.
K.RICHARD   And buried, gentle Tyrrel?
TYRREL   The chaplain of the Tower hath buried them;

But where, to say the truth, I do not know.[151]   30

K.RICHARD Come to me, Tyrrel, soon at after-supper,
When thou shalt tell the process of their death.
Meantime, but think how I may do thee good,
And be inheritor of thy desire.
Farewell till then.

TYRREL   I humbly take my leave.   [*Exit.*

K.RICHARD The son of Clarence have I pent up close;
His daughter meanly have I matched in marriage;
The sons of Edward sleep in Abraham's bosom,[152]
And Anne my wife hath bid this world good night.
Now, for I know the Breton[153] Richmond aims   40
At young Elizabeth, my brother's daughter,
And, by that knot, looks proudly on the crown,
To her go I, a jolly thriving wooer.[154]

Enter RATCLIFFE, *hastily.*[155]

RATCLIFFE My Lord!
K.RICHARD Good or bad news, that thou com'st in so bluntly?
RATCLIFFE Bad news, my lord: Morton is fled to Richmond;[156]
And Buckingham, backed with the hardy Welshmen,
Is in the field, and still his power increaseth.
K.RICHARD Ely with Richmond troubles me more near
Than Buckingham and his rash-levied strength.   50
Come, I have learned that fearful commenting
Is leaden servitor to dull delay;
Delay leads impotent and snail-paced beggary.
Then fiery expedition be my wing,
Jove's Mercury, and herald for a king!
Go, muster men: my counsel is my shield;
We must be brief when traitors brave the field.[157]
                                        [*Exeunt.*

SCENE 4.

London. Before the Palace.

Enter old QUEEN MARGARET.

Q. MARG. So now prosperity begins to mellow
          And drop into the rotten mouth of death.
          Here in these confines slily have I lurked,
          To watch the waning of mine enemies.
          A dire induction am I witness to,
          And will to France, hoping the consequence
          Will prove as bitter, black, and tragical.
          Withdraw thee, wretched Margaret: who comes here?
                                              [*She moves back.*

Enter QUEEN ELIZABETH *and the* DUCHESS OF YORK.

Q. ELIZAB. Ah, my poor Princes! Ah, my tender babes!
            My unblown flowers, new-appearing sweets!   10
            If yet your gentle souls fly in the air
            And be not fixed in doom perpetual,
            Hover about me with your airy wings
            And hear your mother's lamentatiòn!

Q. MARG. [*aside:*] Hover about her; say, that right for right
          Hath dimmed your infant morn to agèd night.[158]

DUCHESS   So many miseries have crazed my voice,
          That my woe-wearied tongue is still and mute.
          – Edward Plantagenet, why art thou dead?

Q. MARG. [*aside:*] Plantagenet doth quit Plantagenet: 20
          Edward for Edward pays a dying debt.[159]

Q. ELIZAB. – Wilt thou, O God, fly from such gentle lambs,
            And throw them in the entrails of the wolf?
            When didst Thou sleep when such a deed was done?

Q. MARG. [*aside:*] When holy Harry died, and my sweet son.[160]

DUCHESS   Dead life, blind sight, poor mortal living ghost,
          Woe's scene, world's shame, grave's due by life
                                                     usurped,[161]
          Brief abstract and recórd of tedious days,
          Rest thy unrest on England's lawful earth,
          Unlawfully made drunk with innocent blood! [*She sits.* 30

Q. ELIZAB.   – Ah, that thou wouldst as soon afford a grave
           As thou canst yield a melancholy seat:
           Then would I hide my bones, not rest them here.
                        [*She sits. The Duchess sits beside her.*
           Ah, who hath any cause to mourn but we?

Q. MARG.   [*advancing:*] If ancient sorrow be most reverend,
           Give mine the benefit of seniory,
           And let my griefs frown on the upper hand.
           If sorrow can admit society,   [*She sits beside them.*
           Tell o'er your woes again by viewing mine:
           I had an Edward, till a Richard killed him,   40
           I had a Harry, till a Richard killed him:
           [*to Eliz.:*] Thou hadst an Edward, till a Richard killed him;
           Thou hadst a Richard, till a Richard killed him.

DUCHESS   I had a Richard too, and thou didst kill him;
           I had a Rutland too: thou holp'st to kill him.

Q. MARG.   Thou hadst a Clarence too, and Richard killed him.[162]
           From forth the kennel of thy womb hath crept
           A hell-hound that doth hunt us all to death:
           That dog, that had his teeth before his eyes,
           To worry lambs and lap their gentle blood;   50
           That foul defacer of God's handiwork;
           That excellent grand tyrant of the earth,
           That reigns in gallèd eyes of weeping souls – [163]
           Thy womb let loose, to chase us to our graves.
           – O upright, just, and true-disposing God,
           How do I thank Thee, that this carnal cur
           Preys on the issue of his mother's body,
           And makes her pew-fellow with others' moan!

DUCHESS   O Harry's wife, triumph not in my woes!
           God witness with me, I have wept for thine.   60

Q. MARG.   Bear with me; I am hungry for revenge,
           And now I cloy me with beholding it.
           Thy Edward he is dead, that killed my Edward;
           Thy other Edward dead, to quit my Edward;
           Young York he is but boot,[164] because both they
           Matched not the high perfection of my loss.
           Thy Clarence, he is dead that stabbed my Edward;
           And the beholders of this frantic play,

Th'adulterate Hastings, Rivers, Vaughan, Grey,
Untimely smothered in their dusky graves.   70
Richard yet lives, Hell's black intelligencer,
Only reserved their factor, to buy souls
And send them thither; but at hand, at hand,
Ensues his piteous and unpitied end:
Earth gapes, Hell burns, fiends roar, saints pray,
To have him suddenly conveyed from hence;
Cancel his bond of life, dear God, I plead,[165]
That I may live and say 'The dog is dead!'.

Q. ELIZAB. O, thou didst prophesy the time would come
That I should wish for thee to help me curse   80
That bottled spider, that foul bunch-backed toad!

Q. MARG. I called thee then 'vain flourish of my fortune';
I called thee then, poor shadow, 'painted Queen',
The presentation of but what I was,
The flatt'ring index of a direful pageant,
One heaved a-high, to be hurled down below,
A mother only mocked with two fair babes;
A dream of what thou wast, a garish flag
To be the aim of every dangerous shot;
A sign of dignity; a breath, a bubble,   90
A queen in jest, only to fill the scene.
Where is thy husband now? Where be thy brothers?
Where be thy two sons? Wherein dost thou joy?
Who sues and kneels and says, 'God save the Queen'?
Where be the bending peers that flattered thee?
Where be the thronging troops that followed thee?
Decline all this, and see what now thou art:
For happy wife, a most distressèd widow;
For joyful mother, one that wails the name;
For Queen, a very caitiff crowned with care;   100
For one being sued to, one that humbly sues;
For she that scorned at me, now scorned of me;
For she being feared of all, now fearing one;
For she commanding all, obeyed of none.
Thus hath the course of justice whirled about,
And left thee but a very prey to time;
Having no more but thought of what thou wast

To torture thee the more, being what thou art.
Thou didst usurp my place, and dost thou not
Usurp the just proportion of my sorrow?   110
Now thy proud neck bears half my burthened yoke,
From which, even here, I slip my weary head,
And leave the burthen of it all on thee.
Farewell, York's wife, and Queen of sad mischance;
These English woes shall make me smile in France.

Q. ELIZAB. O thou well skilled in curses, stay awhile,
And teach me how to curse mine enemies.

Q. MARG. Forbear to sleep the nights, and fast the days;
Compare dead happiness with living woe;
Think that thy babes were sweeter than they were,   120
And he that slew them fouler than he is.
Bett'ring thy loss makes the bad-causer worse;
Revolving this will teach thee how to curse.

Q. ELIZAB. My words are dull; O, quicken them with thine!

Q. MARG. Thy woes will make them sharp and pierce like mine.

                                          [*Exit.*

DUCHESS Why should calamity be full of words?

Q. ELIZAB. Windy attorneys to their clients' woes,
Airy succeeders of intestine joys,
Poor breathing orators of miseries:
Let them have scope. Though what they will impart   130
Help nothing else, yet do they ease the heart.

DUCHESS If so, then be not tongue-tied: go with me,
And in the breath of bitter words let's smother
My damnèd son, that thy two sweet sons smothered.

                                    [*Trumpeting heard.*

The trumpet sounds: be copious in exclaims.

Enter KING RICHARD, CATESBY, *and* SOLDIERS *marching with*
DRUMMERS *and* TRUMPETERS. *The Duchess halts them.*

K.RICHARD Who intercepts me in my expedition?

DUCHESS O, she that might have intercepted thee –
By strangling thee in her accursèd womb –
From all the slaughters, wretch, that thou hast done!

Q. ELIZAB. Hid'st thou that forehead with a golden crown,   140
Where should be branded, if that right were right,
The slaughter of the Prince that owed that crown,

	And the dire death of my poor sons and brothers?	
	Tell me, thou villain slave, where are my children?	
DUCHESS	Thou toad, thou toad, where is thy brother Clarence,	
	And little Ned Plantagenet, his son?	
Q. ELIZAB.	Where is the gentle Rivers, Vaughan, Grey?	
DUCHESS	Where is kind Hastings?	
K. RICHARD	– A flourish, trumpets! Strike alarum, drums!	
	Let not the heavens hear these tell-tale women	150
	Rail on the Lord's anointed: strike, I say!	

                                       [Flourish. Alarums.

	[*To the women:*] Either be patient and entreat me fair,	
	Or with the clamorous report of war	
	Thus will I drown your exclamatìons.	
DUCHESS	Art thou my son?	
K. RICHARD	Ay, I thank God, my father, and yourself.	
DUCHESS	Then patiently hear my impatiènce.	
K. RICHARD	Madam, I have a touch of your condition,	
	That cannot brook the accent of reproof.	
DUCHESS	O, let me speak!	
K. RICHARD	Do then; but I'll not hear.	160
DUCHESS	I will be mild and gentle in my words.	
K. RICHARD	And brief, good mother, for I am in haste.	
DUCHESS	Art thou so hasty? I have stayed for thee,	
	God knows, in torment and in agony.	
K. RICHARD	And came I not at last to comfort you?	
DUCHESS	No, by the Holy Rood, thou know'st it well,	
	Thou cam'st on earth to make the earth my Hell.	
	A grievous burthen was thy birth to me;	
	Tetchy and wayward was thy infancy;	
	Thy school-days frightful, desp'rate, wild, and furious;	170
	Thy prime of manhood daring, bold, and venturous;	
	Thy age confirmed, proud, subtle, sly and bloody,	
	More mild but yet more harmful; kind in hatred.[166]	
	What comfortable hour canst thou name	
	That ever graced me with thy company?	
K. RICHARD	Faith, none, but Humphrey Hour, that called your Grace	
	To breakfast once, forth of my company.[167]	
	If I be so disgracious in your eye,	
	Let me march on, and not offend you, madam.	

	– Strike up the drum!
DUCHESS	I prithee, hear me speak. 180
K.RICHARD	You speak too bitterly.
DUCHESS	Hear me a word,

        For I shall never speak to thee again.

K.RICHARD So?

DUCHESS Either thou wilt die, by God's just ordinance,
        Ere from this war thou turn a conqueror,
        Or I with grief and éxtreme age shall perish
        And never more behold thy face again.
        Therefore take with thee my most grievous curse,
        Which, in the day of battle, tire thee more
        Than all the cómplete armour that thou wear'st.   190
        My prayers on the adverse party fight;
        And there the little souls of Edward's children
        Whisper the spirits of thine enemies
        And promise them success and victory.
        Bloody thou art, bloody will be thy end;
        Shame serves thy life and doth thy death attend. [*Exit.*

Q. ELIZAB. Though far more cause yet much less spirit to curse
        Abides in me, I say 'Amen' to her.

K.RICHARD Stay, madam; I must talk a word with you.

Q. ELIZAB. I have no more sons of the royal blood   200
        For thee to slaughter. For my daughters, Richard,
        They shall be praying nuns, not weeping queens;
        And therefore level not to hit their lives.

K.RICHARD You have a daughter called Elizabeth,
        Virtuous and fair, royal and graciòus.

Q. ELIZAB. And must she die for this? O let her live,
        And I'll corrupt her manners, stain her beauty,
        Slander myself as false to Edward's bed,
        Throw over her the veil of infamy:
        So she may live unscarred of bleeding slaughter,   210
        I will confess she was not Edward's daughter.

K.RICHARD Wrong not her birth, she is a royal princess.

Q. ELIZAB. To save her life, I'll say she is not so.

K.RICHARD Her life is safest only in her birth.[168]

Q. ELIZAB. And only in that safety died her brothers.

K.RICHARD No, at their births good stars were opposite.

Q. ELIZAB. No, to their lives ill friends were contrary.

K.RICHARD All unavoided is the doom of destiny.

Q. ELIZAB. True, when avoided grace makes destiny.[169]
    My babes were destined to a fairer death,   220
    If grace had blessed thee with a fairer life.

K.RICHARD You speak as if that I had slain my cousins!

Q. ELIZAB. Cousins indeed, and by their uncle cozened
    Of comfort, kingdom, kindred, freedom, life.
    Whose hand soever lanced their tender hearts,
    Thy head (all indirectly) gave direction.
    No doubt the murd'rous knife was dull and blunt
    Till it was whetted on thy stone-hard heart
    To revel in the entrails of my lambs.
    But that still use of grief makes wild grief tame,   230
    My tongue should to thy ears not name my boys
    Till that my nails were anchored in thine eyes;
    And I, in such a desp'rate bay of death,
    Like a poor bark, of sails and tackling reft,
    Rush all to pieces on thy rocky bosom.[170]

K.RICHARD Madam, so thrive I in my enterprise
    And dangerous success of bloody wars,
    As I intend more good to you and yours
    Than ever you or yours by me were harmed.

Q. ELIZAB. What good is covered with the face of Heaven,   240
    To be discovered, that can do me good?

K.RICHARD Th'advancement of your children, gentle lady.

Q. ELIZAB. Up to some scaffold, there to lose their heads?

K.RICHARD Unto the dignity and height of fortune,
    The high imperial type of this earth's glory.

Q. ELIZAB. Flatter my sorrow with report of it:
    Tell me what state, what dignity, what honour,
    Canst thou demise to any child of mine?

K.RICHARD Even all I have; ay, and myself and all,
    Will I withal endow a child of thine;   250
    So in the Lethe of thy angry soul
    Thou drown the sad remembrance of those wrongs
    Which thou supposest I have done to thee.

Q. ELIZAB. Be brief; lest that the process of thy kindness
    Last longer telling than thy kindness' date.

K.RICHARD Then know, that from my soul I love thy daughter.

Q. ELIZAB. My daughter's mother thinks it with her soul.

K.RICHARD What do you think?

Q. ELIZAB. That thou dost love my daughter *from* thy soul;
          So *from* thy soul's love didst thou love her brothers;   260
          And *from* my heart's love I do thank thee for it.[171]

K.RICHARD Be not so hasty to confound my meaning:
          I mean that *with* my soul I love thy daughter,
          And do intend to make her Queen of England.

Q. ELIZAB. Well then, who dost thou mean shall be her King?

K.RICHARD Even he that makes her Queen: who else should be?

Q. ELIZAB. What, thou?

K.RICHARD   Even so: how think you of it?

Q. ELIZAB. How canst thou woo her?

K.RICHARD   That would I learn of you,
          As one being best acquainted with her humour.

Q. ELIZAB. And wilt thou learn of me?

K.RICHARD   Madam, with all my heart.   270

Q. ELIZAB. Send to her, by the man that slew her brothers,
          A pair of bleeding hearts; thereon engrave
          'Edward' and 'York'; then haply will she weep.
          Therefore present to her – as sometimes Margaret
          Did to thy father, steeped in Rutland's blood – [172]
          A handkerchief; which, say to her, did drain
          The purple sap from her sweet brother's body,
          And bid her wipe her weeping eyes withal.
          If this inducement move her not to love,
          Send her a letter of thy noble deeds;   280
          Tell her thou mad'st away her uncle Clarence,
          Her uncle Rivers; ay, and for her sake
          Mad'st quick conveyance with her good aunt Anne.

K.RICHARD You mock me, madam. This is not the way
          To win your daughter.

Q. ELIZAB.   There is no other way;
          Unless thou couldst put on some other shape,
          And not be Richard that hath done all this.

K.RICHARD Say that I did all this for love of her.

Q. ELIZAB. Nay, then indeed she cannot choose but hate thee,
          Having bought love with such a bloody spoil.   290

K.RICHARD Look, what is done cannot be now amended.
Men shall deal unadvisedly sometimes,
Which after-hours gives leisure to repent.
If I did take the kingdom from your sons,
To make amends I'll give it to your daughter.
If I have killed the issue of your womb,
To quicken your increase I will beget
Mine issue of your blood upon your daughter.
A grandam's name is little less in love
Than is the doting title of a mother;   300
They are as children but one step below,
Even of your mettle, of your very blood;
Of all one pain, save for a night of groans
Endured of her, for whom you bid like sorrow.
Your children were vexation to your youth,
But *mine* shall be a comfort to your age.
The loss you have is but a son being King,
And by that loss your daughter is made Queen.
I cannot make you what amends I *would*,
Therefore accept such kindness as I *can*.   310
Dorset your son, that with a fearful soul
Leads discontented steps in foreign soil,[173]
This fair alliance quickly shall call home
To high promotions and great dignity:
The King that calls your beauteous daughter 'wife'
Familiarly shall call thy Dorset 'brother'.
Again shall you be mother to a king,
And all the ruins of distressful times
Repaired with double riches of content.
What! We have many goodly days to see: 320
The liquid drops of tears that you have shed
Shall come again, transformed to orient pearl,
Advantaging their loan with interest
Of ten times double gain of happiness.
Go, then, my mother: to thy daughter go;
Make bold her bashful years with your experience;
Prepare her ears to hear a wooer's tale;
Put in her tender heart th'aspiring flame
Of golden sovereignty; acquaint the Princess

   With the sweet silent hours of marriage joys;   330
   And when this arm of mine hath chastisèd
   The petty rebel, dull-brained Buckingham,
   Bound with triumphant garlands will I come
   And lead thy daughter to a conqueror's bed;
   To whom I will retail my conquest won,
   And she shall be sole vict'ress, Caesar's Caesar.
Q. ELIZAB. What were I best to say? Her father's brother
   Would be her Lord? Or shall I say her uncle?
   Or he that slew her brothers and her uncles?
   Under what title shall I woo for thee,   340
   That God, the law, my honour and her love
   Can make seem pleasing to her tender years?[174]
K.RICHARD Infer fair England's peace by this alliance.
Q. ELIZAB. Which she shall purchase with still-lasting war.
K.RICHARD Tell her the King, that may command, entreats.
Q. ELIZAB. That at her hands which the King's King forbids.
K.RICHARD Say she shall be a high and mighty queen.
Q. ELIZAB. To vail the title, as her mother doth.
K.RICHARD Say I will love her everlastingly.
Q. ELIZAB. But how long shall that title 'ever' last?   350
K.RICHARD Sweetly in force unto her fair life's end.
Q. ELIZAB. But how long fairly shall her sweet life last?
K.RICHARD As long as Heaven and nature lengthens it.
Q. ELIZAB. As long as Hell and Richard likes of it.
K.RICHARD Say, I, her sovereign, am her subject low.
Q. ELIZAB. But she, your subject, loathes such sovereignty.
K.RICHARD Be eloquent in my behalf to her.
Q. ELIZAB. An honest tale speeds best being plainly told.
K.RICHARD Then plainly to her tell my loving tale.
Q. ELIZAB. Plain and not honest is too harsh a style.   360
K.RICHARD Your reasons are too shallow and too quick.
Q. ELIZAB. O no, my reasons are too deep and dead:
   Two, deep and dead, poor infants, in their graves.[175]
K.RICHARD Harp not on that string, madam: that is past.
ELIZABETH. Harp on it still shall I, till heart-strings break.
K.RICHARD Now, by my George, my garter,[176] and my crown –
Q. ELIZAB. Profaned, dishonoured, and the third usurped.
K.RICHARD I swear –

Q. ELIZAB.   By nothing; for this is no oath:
              Thy George, profaned, hath lost his lordly honour;
              Thy garter, blemished, pawned his knightly virtue;   370
              Thy crown, usurped, disgraced his kingly glory.
              If something thou wouldst swear to be believed,
              Swear then by something that thou hast not wronged.
K.RICHARD Then, by my self —
Q. ELIZAB.   Thy self is self-misused.
K.RICHARD Now, by the world —
Q. ELIZAB.   'Tis full of thy foul wrongs.
RICHARD   My father's death —
Q. ELIZAB.   Thy life hath it dishonoured.
K.RICHARD Why then, by God —
Q. ELIZAB.   God's wrong is most of all.
              If thou didst fear to break an oath with Him,
              The unity the King my husband made
              Thou hadst not broken, nor my brothers died.   380
              If thou hadst feared to break an oath by Him,
              Th'imperial metal, circling now thy head,
              Had graced the tender temples of my child,
              And both the Princes had been breathing here,
              Which now, two tender bed-fellows for dust,
              Thy broken faith hath made the prey for worms.
              What canst thou swear by now?
K.RICHARD   The time to come.
Q. ELIZAB. That thou hast wrongèd in the time o'erpast;
              For I myself have many tears to wash
              Hereafter time, for time past wronged by thee.   390
              The children live whose fathers thou hast slaughtered,
              Ungoverned youth, to wail it in their age;
              The parents live whose children thou hast butchered,
              Old barren plants, to wail it with their age.
              Swear not by time to come; for that thou hast
              Misused ere used, by times ill-used o'erpast.[177]
K.RICHARD As I intend to prosper and repent,
              So thrive I in my dangerous affairs
              Of hostile arms! Myself myself confound,
              Heaven and fortune bar me happy hours,   400
              Day, yield me not thy light, nor night thy rest,

Be opposite, all planets of good luck,
To my proceeding, if, with dear heart's love,
Immaculate devotion, holy thoughts,
I tender not thy beauteous princely daughter!
In her consists my happiness and thine;
Without her, follows – to myself and thee,
Herself, the land, and many a Christian soul –
Death, desolation, ruin, and decay.
It cannot be avoided but by this;   410
It will not be avoided but by this.
Therefore, dear mother – I must call you so –
Be the attorney of my love to her:
Plead what I will be, not what I have been,
Not my deserts, but what I will deserve;
Urge the necessity and state of times,
And be not peevish found in great designs.

Q. ELIZAB. Shall I be tempted of the Divel thus?
K.RICHARD Ay, if the Divel tempt you to do good.
Q. ELIZAB. Shall I forget myself to be myself?   420
K.RICHARD Ay, if yourself's remembrance wrong yourself.
Q. ELIZAB. Yet thou didst kill my children.
K.RICHARD But in your daughter's womb I bury them:
          Where, in that nest of spicery, they will breed
          Selves of themselves, to your recomforture.
Q. ELIZAB. Shall I go win my daughter to thy will?
K.RICHARD And be a happy mother by the deed.
Q. ELIZAB. I go. Write to me very shortly,
          And you shall understand from me her mind.
K.RICHARD Bear her my true love's kiss [*He kisses her.*]; and so,
                              farewell. [*Exit Queen.* 430
          Relenting fool, and shallow changing woman!

          Enter RATCLIFFE, CATESBY *following.*

          – How now! What news?
RATCLIFFE Most mighty sovereign, on the western coast
          Rideth a puissant navy; to our shores
          Throng many doubtful hollow-hearted friends,
          Unarmed, and unresolved to beat them back.
          'Tis thought that Richmond is their admiral;
          And there they hull, expecting but the aid

Of Buckingham to welcome them ashore.

K.RICHARD Some light-foot friend post to the Duke of Norfolk: 440
Ratcliffe, thyself, or Catesby: where is he?

CATESBY Here, my good Lord.

K.RICHARD Catesby, fly to the Duke.

CATESBY I will, my Lord, with all convenient haste.

K.RICHARD Ratcliffe, come hither! Post to Salisbury:
When thou com'st thither – [*To Catesby:*]
Dull unmindful villain,
Why stay'st thou here, and go'st not to the Duke?

CATESBY First, mighty liege, tell me your Highness' pleasure:
What from your Grace I shall deliver to him.

K.RICHARD O, true, good Catesby: bid him levy straight
The greatest strength and power that he can make, 450
And meet me suddenly at Salisbury.

CATESBY I go. [*Exit.*

RATCLIFFE What, may it please you, shall I do at Salisbury?

K.RICHARD Why, what wouldst thou do there before I go?

RATCLIFFE Your Highness told me I should post before.

K.RICHARD My mind is changed.

Enter STANLEY.

– Stanley, what news with you?

STANLEY None good, my liege, to please you with the hearing;
Nor none so bad, but well may be reported.

K.RICHARD Hoyday, a riddle! Neither good nor bad!
What need'st thou run so many miles about, 460
When thou may'st tell thy tale the nearest way?
Once more, what news?

STANLEY Richmond is on the seas.

K.RICHARD There let him sink, and be the seas on him,
White-livered runagate. What doth he there?

STANLEY I know not, mighty sovereign, but by guess.

K.RICHARD Well, as you guess?

STANLEY Stirred up by Dorset, Buckingham, and Morton,
He makes for England, here to claim the crown.

K.RICHARD Is the chair empty? Is the sword unswayed?
Is the King dead? The empire unpossessed? 470
What heir of York is there alive but we?
And who is England's King but great York's heir?

Then, tell me, what makes he upon the seas?

STANLEY   Unless for that, my liege, I cannot guess.

K.RICHARD Unless for that he comes to be your liege,
           You cannot guess wherefore the Welshman comes.[178]
           Thou wilt revolt and fly to him, I fear.

STANLEY   No, my good Lord; therefore mistrust me not.

K.RICHARD Where is thy power then to beat him back?
           Where be thy tenants and thy followers?   480
           Are they not now upon the western shore,
           Safe-cónducting the rebels from their ships?

STANLEY   No, my good Lord: my friends are in the north.

K.RICHARD Cold friends to me! What do they in the north,
           When they should serve their sovereign in the west?

STANLEY   They have not been commanded, mighty King:
           Pleaseth your Majesty to give me leave,
           I'll muster up my friends, and meet your Grace
           Where and what time your Majesty shall please.

K.RICHARD Ay, ay, thou wouldst be gone, to join with Richmond; 490
           But I'll not trust thee.

STANLEY   Most mighty sovereign,
           You have no cause to hold my friendship doubtful:
           I never was nor never will be false.

K.RICHARD Go then, and muster men; but leave behind
           Your son, George Stanley: look your heart be firm,
           Or else his head's assurance is but frail.

STANLEY   So deal with him, as I prove true to you.   [*Exit.*

                    Enter a MESSENGER.

MESSENGER My gracious sovereign: now in Devonshire,
           As I by friends am well advértisèd,
           Sir Edward Courtney and the haughty prelate,   500
           Bishop of Exeter, his elder brother,
           With many moe confederates, are in arms.

                  Enter another MESSENGER.

MESSENG. 2 In Kent, my liege, the Guildfords are in arms;
           And every hour more competitors
           Flock to the rebels, and their power grows strong.

                  Enter another MESSENGER.

MESSENG. 3 My Lord, the army of great Buckingham —

K.RICHARD Out on you, owls![179] Nothing but songs of death?

　　　　　　　　　　　　　　　　　[*Richard strikes him.*

　　　　　There, take thou that, till thou bring better news.

MESSENG. 3 The news I have to tell your Majesty

　　　　　Is that, by sudden floods and fall of waters,　　　　　510

　　　　　Buckingham's army is dispersed and scattered;

　　　　　And he himself wandered away alone,

　　　　　No man knows whither.

K.RICHARD　　　　　　　　　　　I cry thee mercy:

　　　　　　　　　　　　　　[*Richard gives him a purse.*

　　　　　There is my purse, to cure that blow of thine.

　　　　　Hath any well-advisèd friend proclaimed

　　　　　Reward to him that brings the traitor in?

MESSENG. 3 Such proclamation hath been made, my Lord.

　　　　　　　　　Enter another MESSENGER.

MESSENG. 4 Sir Thomas Lovel and Lord Marquis Dorset,

　　　　　'Tis said, my liege, in Yorkshire are in arms.

　　　　　But this good comfort bring I to your Highness,　　　520

　　　　　The Breton navy is dispersed by tempest:

　　　　　Richmond, in Dorsetshire, sent out a boat

　　　　　Unto the shore, to ask those on the banks

　　　　　If they were his assistants, yea or no;

　　　　　Who answered him, they came from Buckingham

　　　　　Upon his party. He, mistrusting them,

　　　　　Hoist sail and made his course again for Brittany.

K.RICHARD March on, march on, since we are up in arms;

　　　　　If not to fight with foreign enemies,

　　　　　Yet to beat down these rebels here at home.　　　　530

　　　　　　　　　　Enter CATESBY.

CATESBY My liege, the Duke of Buckingham is taken;

　　　　　That is the best news. That the Earl of Richmond

　　　　　Is with a mighty power landed at Milford

　　　　　Is colder tidings; yet they must be told.[180]

K.RICHARD Away towards Salisbury! While we reason here,

　　　　　A royal battle might be won and lost.

　　　　　Some one take order Buckingham be brought

　　　　　To Salisbury; the rest march on with me.

　　　　　　　　　　　　　　　　[*Flourish. Exeunt.*

SCENE 5.

London. Lord Stanley's house.

Enter LORD STANLEY *and* SIR CHRISTOPHER URSWICK, *a priest.*

STANLEY   Sir Christopher, tell Richmond this from me:
That in the sty of the most deadly boar,
My son George Stanley is franked up in hold:
If I revolt, off goes young George's head.
The fear of that holds off my present aid.
So, get thee gone; commend me to thy Lord.
Withal say that the Queen hath heartily consented
He should espouse Elizabeth her daughter.
But, tell me, where is princely Richmond now?

URSWICK   At Pembroke, or at Ha'rford-west, in Wales.   10

STANLEY   What men of name resort to him?

URSWICK   Sir Walter Herbert, a renownèd soldier;
Sir Gilbert Talbot, Sir William Stanley,
Oxford, redoubted Pembroke, Sir James Blunt,
And Rice ap Thomas, with a valiant crew,
And many other of great name and worth;
And towards London do they bend their power,
If by the way they be not fought withal.

STANLEY   Well, hie thee to thy Lord; I kiss his hand.
My letter will resolve him of my mind.   20
Farewell.   [*Exeunt.*

ACT 5, SCENE I.

Salisbury. An open place.

Enter a SHERIFF *with* HALBERDIERS,
leading BUCKINGHAM *to execution.*[181]

BUCKING. Will not King Richard let me speak with him?
SHERIFF No, my good Lord; therefore be patiènt.
BUCKING. Hastings, and Edward's children, Grey and Rivers,
Holy King Henry, and thy fair son Edward,
Vaughan, and all that have miscarrièd
By underhand corrupted foul injustice:
If that your moody discontented souls
Do through the clouds behold this present hour,
Even for revenge mock my destructiòn!
– This is All Souls' Day, fellow, is it not?   10
SHERIFF It is, my Lord.
BUCKING. Why, then All Souls' Day is my body's Doomsday.[182]
This is the day which, in King Edward's time,
I wished might fall on me when I was found
False to his children and his wife's allíes;
This is the day wherein I wished to fall
By the false faith of him whom most I trusted;[183]
This, this All Souls' Day to my fearful soul
Is the determined respite of my wrongs.[184]
That high All-Seer which I dallied with   20
Hath turned my feignèd prayer on my head,
And given in earnest what I begged in jest.
Thus doth He force the swords of wicked men
To turn their own points in their masters' bosoms:
Thus Margaret's curse falls heavy on my neck.
'When he', quoth she, 'shall split thy heart with sorrow,
Remember Margaret was a prophetess.'[185]
– Come, lead me, officers, to the block of shame;
Wrong hath but wrong, and blame the due of blame.
                                                        [*Exeunt.*

SCENE 2.

The camp near Tamworth in Staffordshire.

Enter RICHMOND, *the Earl of* OXFORD, *Sir James* BLUNT, HERBERT,
and SOLDIERS *including a* DRUMMER *and* COLOUR-BEARERS.

RICHMOND   Fellows in arms, and my most loving friends
            Bruised underneath the yoke of tyranny,
            Thus far into the bowels of the land
            Have we marched on without impediment;
            And here receive we from our father Stanley[186]
            Lines of fair comfort and encouragement.
            The wretched, bloody, and usurping boar,
            That spoils your summer fields and fruitful vines,[187]
            Swills your warm blood like wash, and makes his trough
            In your embowelled bosoms: this foul swine   10
            Is now even in the centre of this isle,
            Near to the town of Leicester, as we learn.
            From Tamworth thither is but one day's march.
            In God's name, cheerly on, courageous friends,
            To reap the harvest of perpetual peace
            By this one bloody trial of sharp war.
OXFORD   Every man's conscience is a thousand men
            To fight against this guilty homicide.
HERBERT   I doubt not but his friends will turn to us.
BLUNT   He hath no friends but what are friends for fear,   20
            Which in his dearest need will fly from him.
RICHMOND   All for our vantage. Then, in God's name, march!
            True hope is swift, and flies with swallow's wings;
            Kings it makes gods, and meaner creatures kings.
                                            [*Exeunt, marching.*

SCENE 3.

Bosworth Field, near Market Bosworth in Leicestershire.

Enter, on one side, KING RICHARD *in armour, the* EARL OF SURREY,
the DUKE OF NORFOLK, RATCLIFFE, CATESBY *and* SOLDIERS.

K.RICHARD Here pitch our tent, even here in Bosworth Field.
                               [*Soldiers begin to pitch the tent.*
         – My Lord of Surrey, why look you so sad?
SURREY   My heart is ten times lighter than my looks.
K.RICHARD – My Lord of Norfolk?
NORFOLK   Here, most gracious liege.
K.RICHARD Norfolk, we must have knocks, ha? Must we not?
NORFOLK   We must both give and take, my loving Lord.
K.RICHARD – Up with my tent! Here will I lie tonight;
         But where tomorrow? Well, all's one for that.
         – Who hath descried the number of the traitors?
NORFOLK   Six or seven thousand is their utmost power.   10
K.RICHARD Why, our battalia trebles that account.
         Besides, the King's name is a tower of strength
         Which they upon the adverse faction want.
         – Up with the tent! – Come, noble gentlemen,
         Let us survey the vantage of the ground.
         Call for some men of sound directiòn:
         Let's lack no discipline, make no delay;
         For, Lords, tomorrow is a busy day!   [*Exeunt.*

Enter, on the other side, RICHMOND, SIR WILLIAM BRANDON,
OXFORD, BLUNT, HERBERT *and* SOLDIERS. *Some soldiers pitch
            Richmond's tent opposite Richard's.*

RICHMOND The weary sun hath made a golden set,
         And by the bright tract of his fiery car   20
         Gives token of a goodly day tomorrow.
         – Sir William Brandon, you shall bear my standard.
         – Give me some ink and paper in my tent:
         I'll draw the form and model of our battle,
         Limit each leader to his several charge,
         And part in just proportion our small power.
         – My Lord of Oxford, you, Sir William Brandon,

                And you, Sir Walter Herbert, stay with me.
                The Earl of Pembroke keeps his regiment:
                – Good Captain Blunt, bear my good-night to him,
                And by the second hour in the morning   30
                Desire the Earl to see me in my tent.
                Yet one thing more, good Captain, do for me:
                Where is Lord Stanley quartered, do you know?
BLUNT   Unless I have mistane his colours much
                (Which well I am assured I have not done),
                His regiment lies half a mile, at least,
                South from the mighty power of the King.
RICHMOND If without peril it be possible,
                Sweet Blunt, make some good means to speak
                                                        with him,
                And give him from me this most needful note.   40
BLUNT   Upon my life, my Lord, I'll undertake it;
                And so God give you quiet rest tonight.
RICHMOND Good night, good Captain Blunt.   [*Exit Blunt.*
                                        Come, gentlemen,
                Let us consult upon tomorrow's business.
                Into my tent: the dew is raw and cold.
                    [*Richmond, Brandon, Oxford and Herbert enter the tent.*
                                        The others exeunt.

            Enter, to the King's tent, KING RICHARD, NORFOLK,
                    RATCLIFFE, CATESBY *and* SOLDIERS.

K.RICHARD What is't o'clock?
CATESBY   It's supper-time, my Lord:
                It's nine o'clock.
K.RICHARD   I will not sup tonight.
                Give me some ink and paper.
                What, is my beaver easier than it was?   50
                And all my armour laid into my tent?
CATESBY   It is, my liege; and all things are in readiness.
K.RICHARD – Good Norfolk, hie thee to thy charge;
                Use careful watch, choose trusty sentinels.
NORFOLK   I go, my Lord.
K.RICHARD Stir with the lark tomorrow, gentle Norfolk.
NORFOLK   I warrant you, my Lord.   [*Exit.*
K.RICHARD – Catesby!

CATESBY   My Lord?
K.RICHARD   Send out a pursuivant-at-arms
          To Stanley's regiment; bid him bring his power
          Before sunrising, lest his son George fall
          Into the blind cave of eternal night.   [*Exit Catesby.*   60
          – Fill me a bowl of wine. Give me a watch.
          Saddle white Surrey for the field tomorrow.
          Look that my staves be sound, and not too heavy.
          – Ratcliffe!
RATCLIFFE My Lord?
K.RICHARD Saw'st thou the melancholy Lord Northumberland?
RATCLIFFE Thomas the Earl of Surrey and himself,
          Much about cock-shut time, from troop to troop
          Went through the army, cheering up the soldiers.
K.RICHARD So, I am satisfied. Give me a bowl of wine: 70
          I have not that alacrity of spirit
          Nor cheer of mind that I was wont to have.
                                          [*Wine is brought.*
          Set it down. Is ink and paper ready?
RATCLIFFE It is, my Lord.
K.RICHARD   Bid my guard watch. Leave me.
          Ratcliffe, about the mid of night come to my tent
          And help to arm me. Leave me, I say.
          [*Exeunt Ratcliffe and others. Richard withdraws into his tent*
          (which is guarded by soldiers). He writes, and later sleeps.

          Enter STANLEY *to* RICHMOND *in his tent,*
               LORDS *and* SOLDIERS *attending.*

STANLEY   Fortune and victory sit on thy helm!
RICHMOND All comfort that the dark night can afford   80
          Be to thy person, noble father-in-law![188]
          Tell me, how fares our loving mother?
STANLEY   I, by attorney, bless thee from thy mother,
          Who prays continually for Richmond's good.
          So much for that. The silent hours steal on,
          And flaky darkness breaks within the east.
          In brief, for so the season bids us be,
          Prepare thy battle early in the morning,
          And put thy fortune to th'arbitrement
          Of bloody strokes and mortal-staring war.   90

I, as I may (that which I would I cannot),
With best advantage will deceive the time,[189]
And aid thee in this doubtful shock of arms;
But on thy side I may not be too forward,
Lest, being seen, thy brother, tender George,[190]
Be executed in his father's sight.
Farewell; the leisure and the fearful time[191]
Cuts off the ceremonious vows of love
And ample interchange of sweet discourse
Which so long sundered friends should dwell upon.   100
God give us leisure for these rites of love!
Once more, adieu. Be valiant, and speed well!

RICHMOND – Good Lords, conduct him to his regiment.
I'll strive with troubled thoughts to take a nap,
Lest leaden slumber peise me down tomorrow,
When I should mount with wings of victory.
Once more, good night, kind Lords and gentlemen.
                    [*Exeunt all but Richmond, who kneels.*
O Thou, Whose captain I account myself,
Look on my forces with a gracious eye;
Put in their hands Thy bruising irons of wrath,   110
That they may crush down with a heavy fall
The usurping helmets of our advers'ries.
Make us Thy ministers of chastisement,
That we may praise Thee in the victory.
To Thee I do commend my watchful soul
Ere I let fall the windows of mine eyes:
Sleeping and waking, O, defend me still!
                    [*He lies down and sleeps.*

Enter the GHOST *of* PRINCE EDWARD, *son to Henry VI.*

GHOST   [*to Richard:*] Let me sit heavy on thy soul tomorrow!
Think how thou stab'st me in my prime of youth
At Tewkesbury: despair therefore, and die!   120
[*To Richmond:*] Be cheerful, Richmond; for the
                                            wrongèd souls
Of butchered princes fight in thy behalf:
King Henry's issue, Richmond, comforts thee.   [*Exit.*

        Enter the GHOST *of* KING HENRY VI.

GHOST   [*to Richard:*] When I was mortal, my anointed body
         By thee was punchèd full of deadly holes:
         Think on the Tower and me: despair, and die!¹⁹²
         Harry the Sixth bids thee despair and die!
         [*To Richmond:*] Virtuous and holy, be thou conqueror!
         Harry, that prophesied thou shouldst be King,¹⁹³
         Doth comfort thee in thy sleep: live, and flourish!   130
                                                         [*Exit.*

         Enter the GHOST *of* CLARENCE.

GHOST   [*to Richard:*] Let me sit heavy on thy soul tomorrow!
         I that was washed to death with fulsome wine,
         Poor Clarence, by thy guile betrayed to death.
         Tomorrow in the battle think on me,
         And fall thy edgeless sword: despair, and die!
         [*To Richmond:*] Thou offspring of the House of
                                                         Lancaster,
         The wrongèd heirs of York do pray for thee:
         Good angels guard thy battle! Live, and flourish! [*Exit.*

         Enter the GHOSTS *of* RIVERS, GREY *and* VAUGHAN.

RIVERS   [*to Richard:*] Let me sit heavy on thy soul tomorrow,
         Rivers, that died at Pomfret. Despair, and die!   140
GREY   [*to Richard:*] Think upon Grey, and let thy soul despair!
VAUGHAN [*to Richard:*] Think upon Vaughan, and, with guilty fear,
         Let fall thy lance: despair, and die!
ALL THREE [*to Richmond:*] Awake, and think our wrongs in
                                                 Richard's bosom
         Will conquer him. Awake, and win the day!
                                                 [*Exeunt ghosts.*

         Enter the GHOST *of* LORD HASTINGS.

GHOST   [*to Richard:*] Bloody and guilty, guiltily awake,
         And in a bloody battle end thy days!
         Think on Lord Hastings: despair, and die!
         [*To Richmond:*] Quiet untroubled soul, awake, awake!
         Arm, fight, and conquer, for fair England's sake! [*Exit.* 150

         Enter the GHOSTS *of the two young* PRINCES.

GHOSTS   [*to Richard:*] Dream on thy cousins, smothered in
                                                 the Tower:

Let us be lead within thy bosom, Richard,
And weigh thee down to ruin, shame, and death:
Thy nephews' souls bid thee despair and die!
[*To Richmond:*] Sleep, Richmond, sleep in peace,
                                    and wake in joy;
Good angels guard thee from the boar's annoy!
Live, and beget a happy race of kings!
Edward's unhappy sons do bid thee flourish.

                                    [*Exeunt ghosts.*

          Enter the GHOST *of* LADY ANNE.

GHOST   [*to Richard:*] Richard, thy wife, that wretched
                                    Anne, thy wife,
        That never slept a quiet hour with thee,   160
        Now fills thy sleep with perturbatiòns.
        Tomorrow in the battle think on me,
        And fall thy edgeless sword: despair, and die!
        [*To Richmond:*] Thou quiet soul, sleep thou a
                                    quiet sleep:
        Dream of success and happy victory!
        Thy adversary's wife doth pray for thee.   [*Exit.*

          Enter the GHOST *of* BUCKINGHAM.

GHOST   [*to Richard:*] The first was I that helped thee to
                                    the crown;
        The last was I that felt thy tyranny:
        O, in the battle think on Buckingham,
        And die in terror of thy guiltiness!   170
        Dream on, dream on, of bloody deeds and death;
        Fainting, despair; despairing, yield thy breath!
        [*To Richmond:*] I died for hope ere I could lend
                                    thee aid;[194]
        But cheer thy heart, and be thou not dismayed:
        God and good angels fight on Richmond's side,
        And Richard fall in height of all his pride.   [*Exit.*

          RICHARD *starts to waken.*

K.RICHARD Give me another horse! Bind up my wounds!
        – Have mercy, Jesu! – Soft, I did but dream.
        O coward conscience, how dost thou afflict me!

The lights burn blue.[195] It is now dead midnight.   180
Cold fearful drops stand on my trembling flesh.
What do I fear? Myself? There's none else by.
Richard loves Richard; that is, I am I.
Is there a murtherer here? No; yes, I am:
Then fly. What, from myself? Great reason why –
Lest I revenge. What, myself upon myself?
Alack, I love myself. Wherefore? For any good
That I myself have done unto myself?
O, no. Alas, I rather hate myself
For hateful deeds committed by myself.   190
I am a villain; yet I lie, I am not.
Fool, of thyself speak well; fool, do not flatter.
My conscience hath a thousand several tongues,
And every tongue brings in a several tale,
And every tale condemns me for a villain.
Perjury, perjury, in the high'st degree;
Murther, stern murther, in the dir'st degree;
All several sins, all used in each degree,[196]
Throng to the bar, crying all 'Guilty! Guilty!'.
I shall despair. There is no creature loves me;   200
And if I die, no soul will pity me.
Nay, wherefore should they, since that I myself
Find in myself no pity to myself?
Methought the souls of all that I had murthered
Came to my tent, and every one did threat
Tomorrow's vengeance on the head of Richard.

Enter RATCLIFFE.

RATCLIFFE My Lord!
K.RICHARD Zounds! Who is there?
RATCLIFFE My Lord; 'tis I. The early village cock
     Hath twice done salutation to the morn;   210
     Your friends are up, and buckle on their armour.
K.RICHARD O Ratcliffe, I have dreamed a fearful dream!
     What thinkest thou: will all our friends prove true?
RATCLIFFE No doubt, my Lord.[197]
K.RICHARD   O Ratcliffe, I fear, I fear!
RATCLIFFE Nay, good my Lord, be not afraid of shadows.

K.RICHARD By the apostle Paul, shadows tonight
                    Have struck more terror to the soul of Richard
                    Than can the substance of ten thousand soldiers
                    Armèd in proof and led by shallow Richmond.
                    'Tis not yet near day. Come, go with me;   220
                    Under our tents I'll play the eavesdropper,
                    To hear if any mean to shrink from me.   [*Exeunt.*

           Enter SOLDIERS, *who wait outside Richmond's tent.*
              Enter LORDS *to* RICHMOND, *sitting in his tent.*

LORDS   Good morrow, Richmond!
RICHMOND Cry mercy, Lords and watchful gentlemen,
                    That you have tane a tardy sluggard here!
LORD   How have you slept, my Lord?
RICHMOND The sweetest sleep and fairest-boding dreams
                    That ever entered in a drowsy head
                    Have I since your departure had, my Lords.
                    Methought their souls whose bodies Richard murthered   230
                    Came to my tent and cried on victory.
                    I promise you my soul is very jocund
                    In the remembrance of so fair a dream.
                    How far into the morning is it, Lords?
LORD   Upon the stroke of four.
RICHMOND Why, then 'tis time to arm and give direction.

        He leaves his tent and makes this oration to his soldiers:

                    More than I have said, loving countrymen,
                    The leisure and enforcement of the time
                    Forbids to dwell upon; yet remember this:
                    God and our good cause fight upon our side;   240
                    The prayers of holy saints and wrongèd souls,
                    Like high-reared bulwarks, stand before our faces.
                    Richard except, those whom we fight against
                    Had rather have us win than him they follow:
                    For, what is he they follow? Truly, gentlemen,
                    A bloody tyrant and a homicide;
                    One raised in blood, and one in blood established;
                    One that made means to come by what he hath,
                    And slaughtered those that were the means to help him;
                    A base foul stone, made precious by the foil   250

Of England's chair, where he is falsely set;
One that hath ever been God's enemy.
Then, if you fight against God's enemy,
God will in justice ward you as His soldiers;
If you do sweat to put a tyrant down,
You sleep in peace, the tyrant being slain;
If you do fight against your country's foes,
Your country's fat shall pay your pains the hire;[198]
If you do fight in safeguard of your wives,
Your wives shall welcome home the conquerors;   260
If you do free your children from the sword,
Your children's children quits it in your age.
Then, in the name of God and all these rights,
Advance your standards, draw your willing swords!
For me, the ransom of my bold attempt[199]
Shall be this cold corpse on the earth's cold face;
But if I thrive, the gain of my attempt
The least of you shall share his part thereof.
Sound drums and trumpets boldly and cheerfully;
God and Saint George! Richmond and victory!   270

> [*Drums and trumpets sound. Exeunt Richmond
> and his followers, marching.*

Enter KING RICHARD, RATCLIFFE *and* SOLDIERS.

K.RICHARD What said Northumberland as touching Richmond?
RATCLIFFE That he was never trainèd up in arms.
K.RICHARD He said the truth; and what said Surrey then?
RATCLIFFE He smiled and said, 'The better for our purpose.'
K.RICHARD He was in the right; and so indeed it is. [*A clock strikes.*
Tell the clock there. Give me a calendar.
Who saw the sun today?
RATCLIFFE   Not I, my Lord.
> [*Richard, given an almanac, consults it.*
K.RICHARD Then he disdains to shine; for, by the book,
He should have braved the east an hour ago:
A black day will it be to somebody.   280
– Ratcliffe!
RATCLIFFE My Lord?
K.RICHARD   The sun will not be seen today;

The sky doth frown and lour upon our army.
I would these dewy tears were from the ground.
Not shine today? Why, what is that to me
More than to Richmond? For the selfsame heaven
That frowns on me looks sadly upon him.

Enter NORFOLK *in haste.*

NORFOLK   Arm, arm, my Lord: the foe vaunts in the field!
K.RICHARD Come, bustle, bustle! Caparison my horse!
Call up Lord Stanley, bid him bring his power.
I will lead forth my soldiers to the plain,   290
And thus my battle shall be orderèd:
My foreward shall be drawn out all in length,
Consisting equally of horse and foot;
Our archers shall be placèd in the midst:
John, Duke of Norfolk, Thomas, Earl of Surrey,
Shall have the leading of this foot and horse.
They thus directed, we will follow
In the main battle, whose puissance on either side
Shall be well wingèd with our chiefest horse.
This, and Saint George to boot! What think'st   300
                              thou, Norfolk?
NORFOLK   A good direction, warlike sovereign.
This found I on my tent this morning.

                    [*He shows him a paper.*

K.RICHARD [*reads:*] 'Jockey of Norfolk, be not too bold,
          For Dickon thy master is bought and sold.'²⁰⁰
A thing devisèd by the enemy.
– Go, gentlemen: every man unto his charge.
Let not our babbling dreams affright our souls:
Conscience is but a word that cowards use,
Devised at first to keep the strong in awe.
Our strong arms be our conscience, swords our law!   310
March on, join bravely, let us to't pell-mell:
If not to Heaven, then hand in hand to Hell.

          His oration to his army:

What shall I say more than I have inferred?
Remember whom you are to cope withal:
A sort of vagabonds, rascals, and runaways,

A scum of Bretons and base lackey peasants,
Whom their o'er-cloyèd country vomits forth
To desp'rate adventures and assured destruction.
You sleeping safe, they bring to you unrest;
You having lands, and blest with beauteous wives,   320
They would restrain the one, distain the other.
And who doth lead them but a paltry fellow,
Long kept in Bretagne at our mother's cost?[201]
A milksop, one that never in his life
Felt so much cold as over shoes in snow.
Let's whip these stragglers o'er the seas again,
Lash hence these overweening rags of France,
These famished beggars, weary of their lives,
Who, but for dreaming on this fond explóit,
For want of means, poor rats, had hanged themselves.   330
If we be conquered, let *men* conquer us,
And not these bastard Bretons, whom our fathers
Have in their own land beaten, bobbed, and
                              thumped,
And in recórd left them the heirs of shame.
Shall these enjoy our lands, lie with our wives,
Ravish our daughters? [*Distant drumming.*] Hark! I hear
                              their drum.
Fight, gentlemen of England! Fight, bold yeomen!
Draw, archers, draw your arrows to the head!
Spur your proud horses hard, and ride in blood!
Amaze the welkin with your broken staves!   340

Enter a MESSENGER.

    – What says Lord Stanley? Will he bring his power?
MESSENGER My Lord, he doth deny to come.
K.RICHARD Off with his son George's head!
NORFOLK   My Lord, the enemy is past the marsh:
          After the battle let George Stanley die.
K.RICHARD A thousand hearts are great within my bosom:
          Advance our standards, set upon our foes;
          Our ancient word of courage, fair Saint George,
          Inspire us with the spleen of fiery dragons!
          Upon them! Victory sits on our helms!   350
                    [*Exeunt, soldiers marching.*

SCENE 4.

The same location.

Alarum. Excursions. Enter NORFOLK *and*
SOLDIERS. *Then enter* CATESBY *to him.*

CATESBY   Rescue, my Lord of Norfolk, rescue, rescue!
The King enacts more wonders than a man,
Daring and opposite to every danger:
His horse is slain, and all on foot he fights,
Seeking for Richmond in the throat of death.
Rescue, fair Lord, or else the day is lost!

Alarums. Enter RICHARD.

K.RICHARD A horse! A horse! My kingdom for a horse![202]
CATESBY   Withdraw, my Lord; I'll help you to a horse.
K.RICHARD Slave, I have set my life upon a cast,
And I will stand the hazard of the die.[203]
I think there be six Richmonds in the field;   10
Five have I slain today instead of him.[204]
A horse! A horse! My kingdom for a horse!   [*Exeunt.*

SCENE 5.

The same location.

Alarum. Enter RICHARD *and* RICHMOND; *they fight;*
RICHARD *is slain. A retreat is sounded.*
Exit Richmond. Richard's body is carried off.

A flourish. Enter RICHMOND, STANLEY *(bearing the crown), other*
LORDS, *and* SOLDIERS.

RICHMOND God and your arms be praised, victorious friends!
The day is ours; the bloody dog is dead.
STANLEY   Courageous Richmond, well hast thou acquit thee.
                                        [*He displays the crown.*
Lo, here, this long usurpèd royalty
From the dead temples of this bloody wretch
Have I plucked off, to grace thy brows withal:

Wear it, enjoy it, and make much of it.
[He sets the crown on Richmond's head.[205]

RICHMOND Great God of Heaven, say 'Amen' to all!
– But, tell me, is thy young George Stanley living?

STANLEY He is, my Lord, and safe in Leicester town;
Whither, if it please you, we may now withdraw us.   10

RICHMOND What men of name are slain on either side?

STANLEY John, Duke of Norfolk, Walter, Lord Ferrers,
Sir Robert Brakenbury and Sir William Brandon.

RICHMOND Inter their bodies as become their births.
Proclaim a pardon to the soldiers fled
That in submission will return to us;
And then, as we have tane the sacrament,
We will unite the white rose and the red.[206]
Smile Heaven upon this fair conjunctiòn,
That long have frowned upon their enmity.   20
What traitor hears me and says not 'Amen'?
England hath long been mad, and scarred herself:
The brother blindly shed the brother's blood,
The father rashly slaughtered his own son,
The son, compelled, been butcher to the sire.[207]
All this divided York and Lancaster,
Divided in their dire divisiòn.[208]
O now let Richmond and Elizabeth,
The true succeeders of each royal House,
By God's fair ordinance conjoin together;   30
And let their heirs (God, if Thy will be so,)
Enrich the time to come with smooth-faced peace,
With smiling plenty and fair prosperous days.
Abate the edge of traitors, gracious Lord,
That would reduce these bloody days again
And make poor England weep in streams of blood.
Let them not live to taste this land's increase,
That would with treason wound this fair land's peace!
Now civil wounds are stopped, Peace lives again:
That she may long live here, God say 'Amen'! *[Exeunt.* 40

FINIS

NOTES ON *RICHARD III*

In these notes, the abbreviations include the following:

Bullough: *Narrative and Dramatic Sources of Shakespeare: Volume III: Earlier English History Plays*, ed. Geoffrey Bullough (London: Routledge and Kegan Paul; New York: Columbia University Press; 1960);

e.g.:   *exempli gratia* (Latin): for example;

F1:   the First Folio (1623);

Hall: Edward Hall: *The Union of the Two Noble and Illustrate Famelies of Lancastre and York* (London, 1548);

Holinshed: Raphael Holinshed and others: *The Chronicles of England, Scotland and Ireland*, Vol. III (2nd edn.; London: 1587);

i.e.:   *id est* (Latin): that is;

More: *The Complete Works of St. Thomas More*, Vol. 2, ed. Richard S. Sylvester (New Haven and London: Yale University Press, 1963);

Q1:   the First Quarto (1597);

sc.   scene;

S.D.:   stage-direction.

When quoting the Bishops' Bible, Hall, Holinshed and More, I modernise the spelling and punctuation. In the case of a pun, a metaphor or an ambiguity, the meanings are distinguished as (a) and (b), or as (a), (b) and (c). In other cases, alternative meanings are numbered (i) and (ii).

1 (Title) *THE TRAGEDY ... THIRD*:   In Q1, the first part of the title is: 'The Tragedy of King Richard the third', F1 gives 'The Tragedy of Richard the Third'.

2 (1.1.2) *sun of York;*:   both Q1 and F1 prefer 'son' (Q1 has 'sonne of Yorke'; F1 has 'Son of Yorke'), but 'sun' is indicated by the metaphoric context. A radiant sun was an emblem of

King Edward IV. As the evident pun (a homophone) indicates, Edward was a 'son' of the House of York, as is Richard.

3 (1.1.39-40) 'G' . . . *shall be*.:   An obvious irony: 'G' initiates not only 'George' but also 'Gloucester'. The story of this superstition is told by Hall (Bullough, p. 249.)

4 (1.1.48) *godfathers*.:   traditionally, godfathers were responsible for naming new-born children.

5 (1.1.65) *tempers . . . extremity*.:   F1 has 'tempts him to this harsh Extremity', but the Q1 reading is more authentic and is used here. (Q2 misread 'tempers' as 'tempts', and F1 then added 'harsh' to the transmitted misreading in order to rectify the metre.)

6 (1.1.66-7) *she . . . there*,:   Edward was for a time in love with Elizabeth *née* Woodville, widow of Sir John Grey, and contracted a marriage with her. In F1, 'Woodville' (the family name of Earl Rivers) becomes 'Woodeulle', a botched attempt to indicate locally-trisyllabic pronunciation of a name more usually spelt (as in the quartos) 'Woodvile'. Aurally, the last syllable of line 66 can count as the first syllable of line 67, a line which then, with 'Woodville' stressed on the second syllable, becomes regular.

7 (1.1.73) *Mistress Shore*.:   Jane Shore was the wife of a London goldsmith and a sexual companion of Edward IV. The title 'Mistress' was a term of respect for any woman, married or unmarried.

8 (1.1.81) *widow*:   Elizabeth Woodville, who became Queen Elizabeth when King Edward IV married her.

9 (1.1.112 and S.D.) *Touches . . . weeping*.:   In line 112, 'dearer' is an editorial emendation of 'deeper', which appears in Q1 and F1, but is probably a word contaminated by its echo of 'deep' in line 111. 'Touches me dearer' means (a) 'Affects me more intimately' and (b) 'Implicates me more keenly'. The editorially-supplied stage-direction is prompted by the dialogue at 1.4.234-6.

10 (1.1.115) *I . . . you*,:   'deliver' means 'liberate'; 'lie for you' means (a) 'take your place in the Tower', (b) 'tell lies to help you', and perhaps (c) 'tell lies about you'.

11 (1.1.152-3) *For . . . father?*:   Anne Neville, daughter of the Earl
of Warwick, is treated by Shakespeare as the widow of Prince
Edward (son of Henry VI), who, according to *Henry VI, Part 3*,
Act 5, sc. 5, was slain by Richard and others. (Some scholars
allege that she was only betrothed to Edward, not married to
him; but Shakespeare may be right.) By 'her father', Richard
means her father-in-law, Henry VI, who in *Henry VI, Part 3*,
Act 5, sc. 6, was murdered by Richard.

12 (1.1.155) *her father*::   'the equivalent of her father-in-law, her
king:'

13 (1.2.19) *adders,*:   F1 has 'Wolues, to' (i.e., 'wolves, to'), but
Q1's 'adders' fits better the notion of 'creeping venomed'
creatures.

14 (1.2.27-8) *by the death of him . . . thee!*:   A plausible emendation
of these words would be: 'by the life of him / Than I am by
my young Lord's death and thee!'. The phrase 'by my young
Lord and thee!' means 'by the deaths of Prince Edward and
King Henry VI!'.

15 (1.2.29-30) – *Come, . . . there;*:   Chertsey Abbey was a Bene-
dictine monastery in Surrey; 'Paul's' is St Paul's Cathedral.

16 (1.2.45) *Divel.*:   'Devil'. In the quartos and F1, 'divel' 'Divel',
'divell' and 'Divell' regularly appear, not 'devil' or 'Devil'; so,
to respect Shakespearian sound-patterns, I retain 'Divel' or
'divel' and do not modernise the spelling.

17 (1.2.55-6) *Dead . . . afresh.*:   A superstitious belief was that a
murder-victim's wounds would bleed afresh in the presence of
the murderer.

18 (1.2.73) *O . . . truth!*:   She takes him to mean that he has
denied being man and beast, and therefore must be a devil.

19 (1.2.80) *to accuse*:   The quartos and F1 have 'to curse'; 'to
accuse' is an editorial emendation to harmonise the phrasing
with 'to excuse' in line 82.

20 (1.2.89) *Then . . . slain*::   This is the F1 reading; Q1 has 'Why
then they are not dead,'.

21 (1.2.92-6) *Nay, . . . point.*:   In *Henry VI, Part 3*, Act 5, sc. 5,
Prince Edward is stabbed first by King Edward, then by Richard,
and finally by George, Duke of Clarence. Richard then attempts
to kill Queen Margaret but is restrained by King Edward.

22 (1.2.101) *I . . . yea.*:   Q1 has 'I graunt yea.'; F1 has 'I grant ye.'.

23 (1.2.120) *and . . . effect.*:   Some editors emend the phrase as 'of that accursed effect'; but 'effect' could mean 'entity producing an effect' (as in 'stage effects' or 'alienation effects'). In the next line, Richard uses the noun in the customary sense, 'result'.

24 (1.2.132-3) *Curse . . . thee.*:   He means that she is his day and life; she says she wishes she were his black night and death, to be avenged on him.

25 (1.2.142) *Plantagenet . . . he.*:   Prince Edward was a Plantagenet; so is Richard.

26 (1.2.147) *Never . . . toad.*:   Toads then were wrongly deemed venomous.

27 (1.2.156-60) *No, . . . death,*:   'Edward' is Richard's brother, now the King; Clifford's killing of Rutland is enacted in *Henry VI, Part 3*, Act 1, sc. 3; the 'sad story' of the slaying of the Duke of York is told in *Henry VI, Part 3*, Act 2, sc. 1.

28 (1.2.155-66) *These . . . weeping.*:   These lines, present in F1, were absent from the quarto texts. Perhaps they were cut merely to shorten this long play.

29 (1.2.212) *Crosby House,*:   one of Richard's residences in London.

30 (1.2.226) *Whitefriars;*:   a Carmelite priory in London.

31 (1.2.237) *All . . . nothing!*:   'against enormous odds!'.

32 (1.2.243) *Framed . . . Nature,*:   'formed when Nature was lavish,'.

33 (1.3.20-24) *The Countess . . . arrogance.*:   Stanley's wife, Lady Margaret Beaufort, was, by a former marriage, the mother of Henry Tudor, who would eventually become King Henry VII. As a Lancastrian, she would not have been a friend of the Yorkist King Edward IV or his family.

34 (1.3.37-8) *your . . . Chamberlain;*: 'brothers':   Only one brother, Anthony Woodville, Lord Rivers, appears in the play, but Shakespeare may have thought of this Woodville and Rivers as two characters. The Lord Chamberlain is Hastings.

35 (1.3.41) *at the height.*:   'at the highest point [after which, decline is inevitable, as Fortune turns her wheel].'.

36 (1.3.68-9) *Makes . . . it.*:   Q1 has: 'Makes him to send that thereby he may gather / The ground of your ill will and to

remoue it.'. F1 has: 'Makes him to send, that he may learne the ground.'. The emended version used here derives from Alexander Pope's 1723 edition.

37 (1.3.78) *Our brother*:   George, Duke of Clarence.

38 (1.3.98-100) *marry . . . king,*:   In line 98, 'marry' is the mild oath, 'by the Virgin Mary'; Rivers echoes this sense; but Richard, at 'What, *marry* may she!', uses 'marry' to mean 'wed'.

39 (1.3.114) *Tell . . . said*:   This line is absent from F1 but present in the quartos.

40 (1.3.135-6) *Poor . . . pardon!* –:   Clarence had married Warwick's elder daughter Isabella, sister of Lady Anne, and for a while supported the Lancastrians, but then 'forswore himself' by reverting to the Yorkist side.

41 (1.3.161-2); *If not . . . rebels.*:   'Even if you do not bow like subjects because I am Queen, at least you tremble like rebels because you have deposed me.'

42 (1.3.167-9) *Wert . . . abode.*:   This passage is absent from the quartos but present in F1.

43 (1.3.174-8) *The curse . . . Rutland* –:   This curse was uttered in *Henry VI, Part 3*, Act 1, sc. 4, by Richard Plantagenet, the Duke of York.

44 (1.3.183) *that babe,*:   Rutland, aged 7 at the time of his death.

45 (1.3.210-11) *Rivers and Dorset . . . Hastings,* – :   In *Henry VI, Part 3*, Act 5, sc. 5, Shakespeare had depicted the murder of Edward, Prince of Wales, Lancastrian claimant to the throne, by the Yorkist King Edward, Richard and Clarence; but he had not there specified the presence of Rivers, Dorset and Hastings, though they *were* specified in his sources. The exact circumstances of the killing of Prince Edward at the Battle of Tewkesbury in 1471 remain uncertain.

46 (1.3.228) *hog!*:   Richard's emblem was a white boar, a wild hog.

47 (1.3.256) *Your . . . current.*:   'Your title as peer is so recently conferred that it is hardly recognised, like a newly-minted coin which is scarcely accepted currency.' In fact, Sir Thomas Grey had been given the title of 'Marquess [Marquis] of Dorset' in 1475, and this scene is set in 1483.

48 (1.3.264–5) *Our . . . sun.*:   An eyrie is a nest or brood (here brood) of birds of prey, often eagles: he refers to the sons of York. Ezekiel 17:3 (Bishops' Bible) says that 'a great eagle' took 'the highest branch of the cedar tree'; but, proverbially, 'High cedars fall when low shrubs remain'.

49 (1.3.304) *My hair . . . curses.*:   The quartos ascribe this line to Hastings; F1 ascribes it to Buckingham. As Buckingham has previously remarked that Margaret says nothing that he respects, Hastings seems the more likely speaker here.

50 (1.3, S.D. after 338) *TWO MURDERERS.*:   I allocate the murderers' speeches to, respectively, Murderer 1, Murderer 2, and both murderers. F1's equivalent speech-prefixes are 'Vil.' (for 'Villain', 'Villain' and 'Villains') each time; Q1 has first and secondly 'Execu.' and 'Exec.' (for 'Executioner'), and omits the speech here ascribed to both of them.

51 (1.4, S.D. before line 1) *Enter . . . BRAKENBURY.*:   Q1 has '*Enter Clarence, Brakenbury.*', with Brakenbury acting as Keeper, an economical arrangement. F1 has '*Enter Clarence and Keeper.*', with Brakenbury entering to join them at the line which I number as 76. Various editors preserve the F1 arrangement. In this edition, I prefer Q1's. If Brakenbury enters at 76, his words are peculiarly detached and discourteous: he gives no acknowledgement of the Keeper's presence. Furthermore, if Brakenbury (as Keeper) is present from the start, his reflections at 76–83, on the 'restless cares' of the great, follow naturally from his wish in line 75, 'God give your Grace good rest!'.

52 (1.4.25–6) *Ten . . . pearl,*:   Q1's 'Ten thousand' seems preferable to F1's 'A thousand', for the latter repeats (perhaps accidentally) the 'a thousand' of line 24. In line 26, both Q1 and F1 give 'anchors,'; and editors' emendations, prompted by the context, include 'ingots,' and 'ouches,'. ('Ouches' are brooches.)

53 (1.4.46) *With . . . write of,*:   In the classical afterlife, grim Charon rows the spirits of the newly-dead across the River Styx and/or River Acheron to their underworld abode. The poets mentioned here would include Virgil and Dante.

54 (1.4.49–57) *my great . . . torment!'.*:   Clarence had changed side twice, finally supporting the Yorkists and opposing his father-

in-law, Warwick. The 'shadow' in line 53 is the ghost of Edward, Prince of Wales, son of Henry VI, and Clarence's brother-in-law, murdered by Clarence, Richard and King Edward: see *Henry VI, Part 3*, Act 5, sc. 5. 'Furies' in line 57: in classical mythology, the Furies or Erinyes were three ferocious female deities who avenged crimes, a famous victim being Orestes, a matricide, in Aeschylus's *Oresteia*.

55 (1.4.59) *Environed . . . ears*:   To preserve the pentameter, some editors accentuate 'howled' as 'howlèd'; but this is unnecessary, as 'howled' can naturally be pronounced disyllabically ('how-uld').

56 (1.4.69-72) *O God . . . children!*:   These lines are present in F1 but absent from the quarto texts.

57 (1.4.139-40) *Take . . . sigh.*:   (i:) 'Capture in your mind this devil called "Conscience", and don't believe him: he would like to ingratiate himself with you, but only to cause you grief.' (ii:) 'Let the Devil enter your mind, and do not believe your conscience: conscience would like to ingratiate himself with you, but only to cause you grief.'

58 (1.4.180) *By Christ's . . . sins,*:   This line is absent from F1 (probably as a consequence of the 1606 Act) but present in the quarto texts.

59 (1.4.185-7) *The great . . . murther::*   God's 'Ten Commandments' include 'Thou shalt not kill': Exodus 20:13.

60 (1.4.197) *thy . . . son –*:   Again, Prince Edward, son of King Henry VI.

61 (1.4.227) *And . . . other,*:   This line is absent from F1 but present in the quarto texts.

62 (1.4.247-51) *Which . . . distress.*:   These lines are present in F1 but absent from the quarto texts. F1 gives the last two lines as

> Would not intreat for life, as you would begge
> Were you in my distresse.

Some editors emend these lines substantially (largely because the last line is not a pentameter, i.e. a line with five metrical feet), but I prefer not to. The sense is clear, and this play contains numerous lines which are not in pentameter: the subsequent lines 258 and 263 are examples.

63 (2.1.3-4) *I . . . hence;*:   The 'Redeemer' is, according to
Christian doctrine, God, notably in the form of Jesus Christ,
who by his sacrificial death redeemed his followers from sin
and damnation: see Acts 26:18, for example.

64 (2.1.37) *And . . . friend,*:   To preserve the pentameter, some
editors change 'assured' to 'assurèd'; but this is unnecessary, as
'assured' can naturally be pronounced trisyllabicially (as 'ash-
oo-erd').

65 (2.1.67) *Of you . . . you,*:   Here I follow Q1. F1 offers:

> Of you, and you, Lord *Riuers* and of *Dorset*,
> That all without desert haue frown'd on me:
> Of you, Lord *Wooduill*, and Lord *Scales* of you.

'Wooduill' (or Woodville) was Rivers' family name, and Lord
Scales was one of Rivers' titles. The Q text here corrects errors
that linger in the later F1.

66 (2.1.89) *a wingèd . . . bear;*:   In Roman mythology, Mercury
was the speedy winged messenger of the gods.

67 (2.1.92-5) *God . . . suspiciòn!*:   It is unclear why some who are
'less loyal' and 'nearer in bloody thoughts' should deserve 'not
worse' than Clarence and should 'go current from suspicion'
('circulate freely without being suspected').

68 (2.1.99-100) *Then . . . life,*:   Line 99 appears in Q1 as 'Then
speake at once, what is it thou demandst.'; in F1 it is: 'Then say
at once, what is it thou requests.'. The verb 'demandst' seems
more appropriate to Stanley's tone. As for line 100, the context
shows that his meaning ('The remission, my sovereign, of the
death-sentence on my servant,') is the opposite of what he
appears to say.

69 (2.2. S.D. after 33) *Enter . . . DORSET.*:   Q1 has '*Enter the
Quee.*'; F1 has '*Enter the Queene with her haire about her ears,
Riuers & Dorset after her.*'. In the Elizabethan theatre, dishevelled
hair signified distress.

70 (2.2.40) *Edward . . . dead.*:   In fact, Clarence's death in 1478
preceded the death of Edward IV by five years.

71 (2.2.51) *two . . . semblance*:   Clarence and King Edward.

72 (2.2.89-100) *Comfort . . . throne.*:   This passage appears in F1
but not in the quarto texts.

73 (2.2.117-18) *hearts, . . . together,*: Q1 has 'hearts,'; F1 has 'hates,'. As 'rancour of . . . hates' seems tautological, 'hearts' seems the preferable noun. In line 118, 'splinted' (from quartos 2 to 6, meaning 'set in splints') is obviously preferable to 'splintered' (from the 'splinterd' of Q1 or the 'splinter'd' of F1).

74 (2.2.121) *from Ludlow . . . fet*: Ludlow Castle in Shropshire was the residence of Prince Edward, he being 'Justiciar of Wales' (administrator of part of Wales on behalf of the King) since 1476. (The verb 'fet' means 'fetched.)

75 (2.2.123-40) *Why . . . say I.*: This passage appears in F1 but not in the quarto texts.

76 (2.4.6-7) *But . . . growth.*: At the time of the death of their father, King Edward IV, in April 1483, Edward, Prince of Wales, was 12 year old, and his brother, Richard, Duke of York, was 9.

77 (2.4.21) *And . . . madam.*: F1 ascribes this line to young York; the quartos ascribe it to the Archbishop, and it sounds more like an utterance by the prelate.

78 (2.4.23-5) *Now . . . mine.*: 'Now, by my faith, if I had remembered it at the time, I could have given my gracious uncle an insult to mock his growth more sharply than he mocked mine.'

79 (2.4.36) *Good . . . child.*: F1 ascribes this line to the Duchess; quartos 1-6 ascribe it to the Archbishop. The line is consistent with the Duchess's sympathy with the boy.

80 (2.4.37) *Pitchers . . . ears.*: A version of the proverb, 'Little pitchers have large ears', meaning 'Be careful: youngsters hear and take note'. (The 'ears' of a pitcher, a liquid-container usually made of earthenware, are its handles.)

81 (2.4, S.D. after 37) Enter a *MESSENGER.*: F1 has '*Enter a Messenger.*'; Q1 has '*Enter Dorset.*'.

82 (2.4.41-3) *Lord . . . prisoners.*: This layout follows F1. Q1 offers:

> Dor. Lo: Riuers and Lo: Grey are sent to Pomfret,
> With them, Sir Thomas Vaughan, prisoners.

83 (2.4.51) *jet*: F1 has 'Iutt', i.e. 'jut', meaning 'encroach'; Q1 has 'iet', i.e. 'jet', which can mean both 'encroach' and 'strut', and 'strut' fits the image of 'insulting tyranny'.

84 (2.4.65) *death no more!*: Q1's 'death' fits the context better than the alternative offered by F1, 'earth'.

85 (2.4.66) *sanctuary.*: In England, anyone could claim ecclesiastical sanctuary, which provided immunity to the law (usually with a time-limit). The Queen sought sanctuary at Westminster Abbey. (Ecclesiastical sanctuary was abolished at the Reformation.)

86 (2.4.71) *The Seal I keep;*: The Great Seal of England was the seal used by the monarch to signify his authorisation of important documents. Here the Archbishop is unlawfully surrendering it to a person who is not the reigning monarch or the monarch's authorised keeper of it.

87 (3.1, S.D.) *ACT . . . I.*: The copy-text for this scene until line 165 is Q1. Occasionally, of course, I follow F1.

88 (3.1.1) *Welcome . . . Chamber.*: More, p. 72, refers to London as *camera regis*: the King's Chamber.

89 (3.1.12) *Those . . . dangerous;*: The 'crosses' (i.e. 'setbacks') mentioned in line 4 included the arrest of Rivers, Grey and Vaughan. Rivers was Edward's uncle; Grey was his half-brother.

90 (3.1.69) *Did . . . Lord?*: The oldest part of the Tower of London is the White Tower, founded by William the Conqueror. There was a legend that a fort built by Julius Caesar had stood on the same site. The original tower was protected on two sides by the Roman walls of the city.

91 (3.1.82-3) *Thus, . . . word.*: 'Thus, like the conventional Vice, Iniquity, in the Morality Plays, in one word I combine different moral meanings.' In fact, here he has not done that; he has simply given a lying answer. 'Iniquity' is a character in the plays *Nice Wanton* and *King Darius*: there he tells lies but is not notably ambiguous.

92 (3.1.85-6) *With . . . live.*: 'The valorous deeds that enriched his mind lived on because he was minded to record them.'

93 (3.1.92) *our . . . again,*: The French throne was claimed by Henry V and Henry VI.

94 (3.1.94) *Short . . . spring.*:   'An early spring easily results in a short summer.' In other words, 'A precocious lad like this aspiring Prince is asking for trouble: quite likely he won't live long.'

95 (3.1.114) *It . . . give.*:   'It being' emends Q1's 'And being'.

96 (3.1.121) *I'd . . . heavier.*:   (i) 'If it were heavier, I would wear it readily'; (ii) 'Even if it were heavier, I would deem it trivial.' The 'I'd' emends Q1's 'I'.

97 (3.1.130–31) *Because . . . shoulders.*:   Dr Johnson claimed that, at country shows, an ape was set on a bear's shoulder; and a painting by Holbein depicts a Fool (Will Somers) carrying a monkey on his left shoulder. Buckingham's subsequent comment seems to suggest that the Prince is mocking himself (as a little ape) rather than Richard (as bear or Fool); but Buckingham is mollifying or ironic.

98 (3.1.157–8) *Well, . . . intend,*:   I emend Q1's 'Well, let them rest: Come hither Catesby, / Thou art sworne as deeply to effect what we intend,'.

99 (3.1.171–5) *How . . . reasons;*:   After 'purpose,', Q1 has 'if he be willing, / Encourage him, and shew him all our reasons:'. I follow F1.

100 (3.1.179) *divided Councils,*:   One Council meeting will be public, to plan the Prince's coronation; the other will be private, to plot Richard's seizure of the crown.

101 (3.1.181–5) *Commend . . . more.*:   'Lord William' is Hastings; 'ancient knot' means 'long-established clique'; and 'are let blood': means 'undergo blood-letting', a surgical euphemism for 'are executed'. After King Edward's death, Jane Shore ('Mistress Shore') became, in turn, Hastings' mistress (according to More, p. 48).

102 (3.1.193) *Chop . . . determine.*:   Q1 has 'Chop of his head man, somewhat we will doe;', while F1 has 'Chop off his Head: / Something wee will determine:'.

103 (3.1.200) *We . . . form.*:   'We may render our plots more orderly' (punning on 'digest', meaning both 'absorb food' and 'order, arrange, summarise').

104 (3.2.11) *He . . . helm;*: 'He dreamt the boar had sheared off his helmet;': tantamount to dreaming that Richard, whose emblem is the boar, had cut off his head.

105 (3.2.58) *they . . . hate,*: 'those (Rivers, Vaughan and Grey) who turned King Edward against me,'.

106 (3.2.69–70) *The Princes . . . Bridge.*: 'The Princes both esteem you highly (for they count on seeing your severed head displayed on high at London Bridge, where traitors' heads are exposed on poles).'

107 (3.2.86) *This . . . misdoubt:*: 'I fear a sudden malicious blow (like this that struck Rivers, Vaughan and Grey):'.

108 (3.2.88) *The day is spent.*: The usual meaning would be 'The day is ending'; but this scene opened 'Upon the stroke of four [a.m.]'. In Shakespeare's *Venus and Adonis*, line 717, the clause 'The night is spent' appears to mean 'The night is well under way'; so here the sense 'The day is well under way' is plausible (particularly given the frequent fluidity of time in Shakespearian drama).

109 (3.2, S.D. after 93) *PURSUIVANT.*: A pursuivant is a messenger authorised to serve warrants. According to the quarto texts, this character bears, coincidentally, the surname Hastings (as he did in Holinshed).

110 (3.3, S.D. before line 1) *Enter . . . death.*: This S.D. is based on that in F1. In Q1, the S.D. ('*Enter Sir Richard Ratliffe, with the Lo: Riuers, Gray, and Vaughan, prisoners.*') is followed by this line of dialogue:

    Ratl. Come bring foorth the prisoners.

This line does not fit either S.D., each of which specifies that the prisoners have already been brought forth. I therefore omit it.

111 (3.3.12) *And, . . . seat,*: 'and, to add a further insult to this dismal place,'.

112 (3.3.14–18) *Now . . . Hastings.*: In Act 1, sc. 3, Margaret cursed Hastings, Rivers, Dorset, Richard, Buckingham and Grey (see lines 210–14, 217–21 and 297–303: 302–3 include Grey).

113 (3.4, S.D. before 1) *Enter . . . table.*: F1 says that Ratcliffe is present in this scene; but, as he is in Pomfret, I delete him. Q1

excludes Ratcliffe and names Catesby, so I include Catesby. Towards the end of the scene, in the F1 version, Buckingham is guarded by Lovel and Ratcliffe; but in the Q1 version, he is guarded only by Catesby. I follow Q1.

114 (3.4.31-2) *My . . . there*:: Reputedly, the best strawberries in England were those grown in the gardens of the Bishop of Ely's palace in the Holborn district of London. A strawberry fair is said to have been held there in mediaeval times, and a fair continued to be held in the 21st century.

115 (3.4.55) *livelihood*: Q1 has 'likelihood' ('appearance'); F1 has 'liuelyhood', i.e. 'livelihead' ('animation'). One editorial theory is that 'likelihood' results from a 'foul-case error', the physical letter 'k' having been wrongly placed by the compositor in the box for 'v'.

116 (3.4.67-71) *Look . . . me.*: Thomas More (p. 48) says that the observers knew well that Richard's arm had been withered from birth. (See *Henry VI, Part 3*, Act 3, sc. 3.) More also states that the Queen, too wise for such folly, would never have conspired with Shore's wife, whom she hated. But the parliamentary Bill requesting Richard to take the throne cited 'sorcery and witchcraft, committed by the said Elizabeth and her mother Jacquetta, Duchess of Bedford': *Rotuli Parliamentorum*, Vol. VI, p. 241.

117 (3.4.101-4) *Come, . . . upon.*: These lines are present in F1 but absent from the quartos.

118 (3.5, S.D. before line 1) Enter . . . armour.: The S.D. in F1 is: '*Enter Richard, and Buckingham, in rotten Armour, maruellous ill-fauoured.*'. More (pp. 52-3) explains that Richard and Buckingham wore the rusty armour to support their allegation that they had been the victims of a sudden attack by Hastings and other conspirators, forcing them to seize the first armour to hand, which happened to be old gear. They had repelled the conspirators, they claimed. More (p. 53) adds that nobody believed the allegation. In 3.5.14-19, Richard and Buckingham seek to create the illusion that a further attack may be imminent. As the F1 version of this scene features Ratcliffe, though he was at Pomfret, I follow the Q1 version of this scene, which differs in many particulars from F1's.

119 (3.5.11) *stratagems.*:   In F1, the dialogue continues thus:

[*Buck.*] But what, is *Catesby* gone?
Rich.   He is, and see he brings the Maior along.
                Enter the Maior, and Catesby.
Buck.   Lord Maior.
Rich.   Looke to the Draw-Bridge there.
Buck.   Hearke, a Drumme.
Rich.   *Catesby*, o're-looke the Walls.
Buck.   Lord Maior, the reason we haue sent.
Rich.   Looke back, defend thee, here are Enemies.
Buck.   God and our Innocencie defend, and guard vs.
        Enter Louell and Ratcliffe, with Hastings Head.
Rich.   Be patient, they are friends: *Ratcliffe*, and *Louell.*

120 (3.5.48-59) *I never . . . death.*:   F1 assigns these lines to Buckingham.

121 (3.5.71) *Guildhall*:   the location of municipal government in London.

122 (3.5.74-7) *Tell . . . so.*:   More, as reported by Hall, says that a citizen, Burdet, who owned a house called 'The Crown', declared that his son would inherit it. King Edward, hearing of this, thought that he was referring to the royal crown, i.e. the monarchy, and had the citizen hideously killed (drawn and quartered). (See Bullough, p. 273.)

123 (3.5.101) *Now . . . order.*:   In F1, this line is preceded by the following three lines from Richard:

> Goe *Louell* with all speed to Doctor *Shaw*,
> Goe thou to Fryer *Peuker*, bid them both
> Meet me within this houre at Baynards Castle.

Baynard's Castle was the London residence of the Duchess of York.

124 (3.6.11) *palpable device?*:   A 'palpable device' is an obvious trick, the trick here being that the report of Hastings' alleged attack on Richard and Buckingham (a report used to justify his execution) had been written well in advance of the time when Hastings was supposed to have made that attack.

125 (3.6.13-14) *all . . . thought.*:   'all will come to ruin, when such wicked contrivances must only be observed in thoughts [and

not spoken about].' Fi gives 'nought' (i.e. 'nothing'), which I render freely as 'ruin'; Qi gives 'naught', which can mean 'wickedness'.

126 (3.7.5-6) *his . . . France;*:   More (pp. 62-5) says that when King Edward IV was wooing Elizabeth Grey, he was thought to be already betrothed to Lady Elizabeth Lucy, whom he had impregnated. (Lady Elizabeth Lucy, however, denied that there was a betrothal, though she said she had hoped to marry him.)   Edward also, in vain, had attempted to enter a proxy marriage contract with Bona of Savoy, sister-in-law of the French King. (See *Henry VI, Part 3*, Act 3, scenes 2 and 3.) Richard and Buckingham allege that marriage contracts had been agreed in both cases, and that Edward's subsequent marriage to Elizabeth Grey was invalid, rendering the children of that marriage illegitimate. (Incidentally, lines 5-6, 8 and 11 are present in Fi but absent from the quarto texts.)

127 (3.7.9) *tyranny for trifles;*:   'tyrannical wrath over trivial matters': as when Edward had Burdet killed: see note 122.

128 (3.7.15) *victories in Scotland.*:   In 1482 Richard had campaigned successfully against the Scots, capturing Berwick, and later taking Edinburgh without the loss of a single man. Parliament congratulated him in 1483.

129 (3.7.25) *statuas*:   In Qi and Fi, the word 'Statues' is trisyllabic: hence my emendation of the spelling. 'Statuas' (recalling the Latin 'statua' for 'statue') gives clearer utterance than 'statuès'.

130 (3.7.30) *To . . . Récorder.*:   'Recorder' could be stressed on the first syllable, which regularises the metre. (Gary Taylor, an editor, prefers to add 'so' before 'spoke'.) The 'Recorder' was the chief legal official at the court of the Lord Mayor and aldermen of London.

131 (3.7.139) *And . . . instigatiòn,*:   Qi and Fi have 'And by their vehement instigation,'. My emendation, showing that 'instigation' has here five syllables, clarifies the pentameter. ('Vehement instigation' means 'fervent advocacy'.)

132 (3.7.144-53) *If . . . you:*:   This passage appears in Fi but not in the quarto texts.

133 (3.7.179) *Lucy*: According to More (pp. 64-5), Edward's mother was so troubled by his liaison with Elizabeth Lucy that she felt that his marriage to Elizabeth Grey should not proceed until this obstacle was 'purged' and the truth openly acknowledged.

134 (3.7.183) *petitioner,*: Elizabeth Grey had petitioned King Edward for the return of her late husband's lands. (See More, p. 60, and *Henry VI, Part 3*, Act 3, sc. 2.)

135 (3.7.177-91) *You . . . Prince'.*: Buckingham cites Edward's alleged marriage contracts to Lady Elizabeth Lucy and to Princess Bona of Savoy, the French King's sister-in-law, to argue that the marriage to Elizabeth Grey was bigamous and the offspring illegitimate. More (p. 64) says that Edward remarked: 'As for the bigamy, . . . I understand it is forbidden a priest, but I never wist [knew] it yet that it was forbidden a prince.'

136 (4.1.1-2) *my niece Plantagenet, . . . aunt of Gloucester?*: Actually, Margaret Plantagenet, Clarence's daughter, was the Duchess of York's grand-daughter. The 'aunt of Gloucester' is Lady Anne, Duchess of Gloucester. Later, at line 5, Anne is addressed as the Duchess of York's daughter, but was her daughter-in-law. At line 7, Anne, addressed as Elizabeth's sister, was her sister-in-law.

137 (4.1.1-7) *Who . . . away?*: This passage is represented in Q1 by just two lines:

> *Duch.* Who meets vs here, my neece Plantagenet?
> *Qu.* Sister well met, whether awaie so fast?

138 (4.1.29-30) *I'll . . . Queens.*: By 'mother', he means 'mother-in-law'. The 'Queens' are Elizabeth, widow of Edward IV, and Anne, wife of Richard (who is about to be crowned as King Richard III).

139 (4.1.42) *And . . . Hell:*: Henry Tudor, Earl of Richmond (later Henry VII) had sought refuge in Brittany.

140 (4.1.49) *son*: probably referring to his stepson, Richmond; possibly referring to his son, George.

141 (4.1.97-103) *Stay, . . . farewell.*: This passage appears in F1 but not in the quartos.

142 (4.2.8) *play the touch*,: 'assume the function of a touchstone' (used for assessing the quality of gold).

143 (4.2.50-52) *Rumour . . . close.*: Hall's *Union* (Bullough, pp. 287-8) says that Richard, in order to accelerate Queen Anne's death, initiated the rumour that she had died; hearing of this, she was greatly distressed; and, soon, she did die, either from 'inward thought and pensiveness of heart' or by 'intoxication of poison' (the latter said to be more likely). 'I will take order for her keeping close' means 'I will arrange to have her kept out of sight'.

144 (4.2.53-5) *Inquire . . . him.*: Clarence's daughter, Margaret Plantagenet (1473-1541), married Sir Richard Pole, cousin of Henry VII. The 'boy' is Clarence's eldest son, Edward, Earl of Warwick (1475-99). From 1485 to 1499 he was held prisoner in the Tower of London; in 1499 he was executed. Hall says that he 'could not discern a Goose from a Capon', but that was after years of imprisonment.

145 (4.2.60) *my brother's daughter*,: Edward IV's daughter, Elizabeth of York. In 1486, however, she married Henry Tudor, Earl of Richmond (subsequently King Henry VII), thus uniting the houses of York and Lancaster.

146 (4.2.86) *son*:: Richmond.

147 (4.2.94-6) *I do . . . boy.*: This prophecy was uttered in *Henry VI, Part 3*, Act 4, sc. 6.

148 (4.2.101-5) *Richmond! . . . Richmond.*: Shakespeare's source for this story was Holinshed (pp. 745-6). Irish bards were sometimes deemed to have prophetic powers.

149 (4.2.111-13) *Because . . . today.*: A 'Jack' is a mechanical man who, on some clocks, appears to strike the bell to mark the time. Buckingham's repeated request interrupts the King's 'meditation'. Lines 98-113 of this scene are present in Q1 but not in F1.

150 (4.2.119) *Brecknock*,: Buckingham resided at Brecknock Castle in Brecon, Wales.

151 (4.3.29-30) *The chaplain . . . know.*: In 1674, workmen at the Tower of London uncovered a wooden chest containing the skeletons of two children. The bones, assumed to be those of

the two princes, were placed in an urn which was then displayed in Westminster Abbey.

152 (4.3.36-8) *The son . . . bosom,*:   Edward Plantagenet, Earl of Warwick, was a potential claimant to the throne. He was kept in confinement by both Richard and, later, Henry VII, who executed him in 1499. Margaret Plantagenet, who married Sir Richard Pole, was executed by Henry VIII in 1541. Possibly Shakespeare confused her with her first cousin, Princess Cicely, whom (Holinshed says, p. 752,) Richard married to 'a man . . . of an unknown lineage'. (Eventually, Cicely had three marriages.) Sir Richard Pole had a distinguished and successful career. Edward IV's sons, Prince Edward (the uncrowned King) and Richard, Duke of York, have just been slain in the Tower. (To 'sleep in Abraham's bosom' means to 'be in Heaven': see Luke 16: 22-3.)

153 (4.3.40) *Breton*:   This is a common clarificatory emendation of F1's 'Britaine' (and Q1 has 'Brittaine'). Richmond (no Breton) was in exile in Brittany.

154 (4.3.39-43) *Anne . . . wooer.*:   Having effected the death of his wife, Richard plans to marry his niece Elizabeth (sister to the slain young princes) in order to strengthen his dynastic position. The plan looks incestuous, but the Church could issue a dispensation in some such cases.

155 (4.3, S.D. after 43) *Enter . . . hastily.*:   Q1 has Catesby entering here; F1 has Ratcliffe. I assume that audiences will permit Ratcliffe to have returned from Pomfret by this time. My '*hastily*' is an inference from Richard's reference to his 'blunt' arrival.

156 (4.3.46) *Morton . . . Richmond;*:   The 'Morton' is John Morton, Bishop of Ely.

157 (4.3.56-7) *my counsel . . . field.*:   'my shield serves as my advisor: we need few words when traitors are already displaying themselves defiantly on the battlefield.'

158 (4.4.15-16) *right . . . night.*:   'retributive justice has changed your youthful morning into the long night of death.'

159 (4.4.20-21) *Plantagenet doth . . . debt.*:   'A Plantagenet pays for a Plantagenet: Prince Edward (Elizabeth's son) pays in death for the death of Prince Edward (Margaret's son).'

160 (4.4.25) *When . . . son.*: 'holy Harry' is Henry VI (her husband); Prince Edward is her son.

161 (4.4.27) *grave's . . . usurped,*: 'one who should be dead but is wrongly retained by life'. In lines 26-30, she is apparently addressing Elizabeth, who responds in line 33 to the proposal in line 29 that she should sit.

162 (4.4.40-46) *I had . . . him.*: In line 40, the Edward is Margaret's son, killed by Richard and his brothers at Tewkesbury (see *Henry VI, Part 3*, Act 5, sc. 3). In 41, 'Harry' is Henry VI, killed by Richard in the Tower (see *Henry VI, Part 3*, Act 5, sc. 6). In 42, 'Edward' is Elizabeth's older son, whose killing in the Tower was ordered by Richard. In 43, 'Richard' is her younger son, also killed in the Tower. In 44, 'Richard' is the Duchess's husband, Richard, Duke of York, killed by Margaret and Clifford (see *Henry VI, Part 3*, Act 1, sc. 4). In 45, 'Rutland' is the Duchess's son, killed by Clifford (see *Henry VI, Part 3*, Act 1, sc. 3). In 46, 'Clarence' is Richard's brother, recently killed by Richard's command (Act 1, sc. 4).

163 (4.4.51-3) *That foul . . . souls –*: Q1 omits our lines 52-3; F1 puts our 53 before our 52.

164 (4.4.63-5) *Thy . . . boot,*: 'Thy Edward' is Edward IV; 'Thy other Edward' is Edward V; 'York' is Elizabeth's second son, the young Duke of York; 'but boot' means 'just a make-weight'.

165 (4.4.77) *plead,*: Although both Q1 and F1 have 'pray,' a tempting emendation is 'plead,'. Substitution of 'plead,' averts the repetition of 'pray,' and (now making only an eye-rhyme) formerly would have made a true rhyme with 'dead': which would be appropriate, since Margaret's next long speech ends in a rhyming couplet.

166 (4.4.173) *kind in hatred.*: 'appearing kind when hating.'.

167 (4.4.176-7) *Hour . . . company.*: In line 176, 'Hour' has one syllable, but, at line 174, 'hour' is disyllabic, to preserve the pentameter. 'Hour' is also disyllabic at 4.4.504. 'Humphrey Hour' ('Hower' in F1) remains unidentified.

168 (4.4.214) *Her . . . birth.*: 'Her life is safe only because she is nobly born.'

169 (4.4.219) *when . . . destiny.*:   'when a man who has rejected God's grace (Richard) decides the fate of people.'.

170 (4.4.222-35) *You . . . bosom.*:   These lines appear in F1 but not in the quartos.

171 (4.4.256-61) *from . . . for it.*:   Richard's 'from my soul' means 'with my soul'. Queen Elizabeth employs '*from*' to mean 'apart from'.

172 (4.4.274-5) *as . . . blood* −:   This incident was enacted in *Henry VI, Part 3*, Act 1, sc. 4.

173 (4.4.311-12) *Dorset . . . soil,*:   Dorset fled from Richard to Yorkshire, took part in Buckingham's unsuccessful rising, and travelled to Brittany, where he joined Richmond. (Shakespeare will locate him in the Battle of Bosworth, but in fact Dorset did not return to England until recalled by Henry VII.)

174 (4.4.288-342) *Say . . . years?*:   These lines appear in F1 but not in the quartos.

175 (4.4.361-3) *Your . . . graves.*:   By 'quick', Richard means 'hasty'. Elizabeth, taking it to mean 'alive', responds that her 'reasons' are 'dead': they are the murdered princes. Her 'too' in line 362 punningly evokes the 'two,' (as my emendation makes explicit) in line 363.

176 (4.4.366) *Now, . . . garter,*:   The insignia of the Order of the Garter, the highest order of knighthood, included a garter and a jewelled pendant bearing the image of Saint George.

177 (4.4.395-6) *for . . . o'erpast.*:   'because you have marred it before it has been traversed, your bad deeds of former times having overshadowed it.'

178 (4.4.474-6) *Unless . . . comes.*:   Stanley's 'Unless for that' means 'In the absence of such conditions' (e.g. an empty throne). Taking 'Unless for that' to mean 'Unless because', Richard twists Stanley's words into a declaration of disloyalty. (Richmond is 'the Welshman' because of his descent from the Welsh Owen Tudor.)

179 (4.4.507) *owls!*:   An owl's mournful cry supposedly foretold death.

180 (4.4.498–534) *My . . . told.*:   Shakespeare combines Hall's accounts of (i) Richmond's abortive attempt to invade England and join Buckingham (in 1483) and (ii) his successful invasion (in 1485).

181 (5.1, S.D. before line 1) *execution.*:   Historically, Buckingham's execution took place in 1483, more than 21 months before the Battle of Bosworth.

182 (5.1.10–12) *All-Souls' Day . . . Doomsday.*:   All-Souls' Day, November 2, is the day when the Roman Catholic Church intercedes for all Christian souls, and when ghosts were thought to walk the earth. Doomsday, according to the Church, is the day of the Last Judgement of all souls: for instance, souls previously assigned to Purgatory will then go to Heaven.

183 (5.1.13–17) *This . . . trusted;*:   See his prophecy in 2.1.32–40.

184 (5.1.19) *Is . . . wrongs.*:   'is the preordained ending of my wrong-doing.'.

185 (5.1.26–7) *'When . . . prophetess.'*:   See 1.3.299–301.

186 (5.2.5) *our father Stanley*:   Richmond employs the royal plural. Stanley was his stepfather.

187 (5.2.7–8) *The . . . vines,*:   The imagery associates Richard, whose emblem was a boar, with the goddess Diana's boar, which ravaged cornfields and vineyards (see Ovid's *Metamorphoses*, Book 8).

188 (5.3.81) *father-in-law!*:   stepfather.

189 (5.3.92) *With . . . time,*:   'as ably as opportunity permits, will practise trickery,'. This speech implies that Stanley's forces will covertly help Richmond; certainly Stanley will refuse to fight for Richard, though Richard was relying on his support.

190 (5.3.95) *brother . . . George,*:   George was Richmond's step-brother.

191 (5.3.97) *the leisure . . . time*:   Here and at line 238, 'the leisure' means its opposite, 'the lack of leisure'; contrast the leisure envisaged in line 101.

192 (5.3.126) *despair, . . . die!*:   Each of the ghosts urges Richard to commit the mortal sin of despair, associated with Judas.

193 (5.3.129) *Harry, . . . King,*:   The prophecy was made in
    Henry VI, Part 3, Act 4, sc. 6:   'This pretty lad will prove our
    country's bliss', etc.

194 (5.3.173) *I . . . aid;*:   Editorial interpretations range from 'I
    despaired before I could aid you;' to 'I died before I could
    give you help, yet hoping that I could help you;'.

195 (5.3.180) *The lights burn blue.*:   a sign that ghosts are present.

196 (5.3.198) *each degree,*: each level of infamy, from bad to worst.

197 (5.3.212-14) *O . . . Lord.*:   These lines are present in the
    quarto texts but absent from F1.

198 (5.3.258) *Your . . . hire;*:   'Your country's surplus wealth will
    reward your efforts;'.

199 (5.3.265) *the ransom . . . attempt*:   'the penalty for my bold
    endeavour (if I fail)'.

200 (5.3.304-5) *'Jockey . . . sold.'*:   According to Hall (Bullough,
    p. 297), John, Duke of Norfolk, received various warnings
    not to fight for Richard, one being this message in doggerel
    verse. 'Jockey' and 'Dickon' further nickname 'Jonkin' (for
    'Little John') and 'Dick' (Richard).

201 (5.3.324) *Long . . . mother's cost?*:   Shakespeare was misled by
    a misprint in the second edition (1587) of Holinshed, which
    substituted 'mother's' for 'brother's'. Richard's brother-in-
    law, Charles, Duke of Burgundy, had long supported the
    exiled Richmond. ('Bretagne', for 'Brittany', is a metrically-
    apt editorial clarification of the 'Brittaine' found in the quarto
    texts and F1.) Richmond's troops included Bretons, former
    English exiles, and French, Scottish and Welsh soldiers.

202 (5.4.7) *A horse! . . . horse!*:   In the anonymous *The True
    Tragedy of Richard III* (1594), Richard, wounded in the battle,
    cries 'A horse, a horse, a fresh horse', and refuses to flee.

203 (5.4.9-10) *I have . . . die.*:   'I have risked my life on one
    throw of the die, and I will respect the chance outcome of its
    fall.' ('Die' is the singular of 'dice'.)

204 (5.4.11-12) *I think . . . him.'*:   Leaders in battle would
    sometimes arrange for other fighters to resemble them, a
    protective stratagem. In *Henry IV, Part 1*, Act 5, sc. 4, Douglas
    encounters numerous 'counterfeits' of King Henry.

205 (5.5, S.D. after line 7:) *[He . . . head.*:   Richmond is now *de facto* monarch, so some editors let his speech-prefix hereafter be 'KING HENRY VII'. As he still refers to himself as 'Richmond' (in line 29), I respect his usage.

206 (5.5.18-19) *And . . . red.*:   Richmond, at Rheims, had taken an oath that, when he was crowned, he would marry Elizabeth. The marriage of the Lancastrian Richmond and the Yorkist Elizabeth ended the Wars of the Roses, dramatised in the *Henry VI* plays.

207 (5.5.25-6) *The father . . . sire.*:   These events were enacted in *Henry VI, Part 3*, Act 2, sc. 5.

208 (5.5.27-8) *All . . . divisiòn.*:   'All this divided the Houses of York and Lancaster: there were even further (familial) divisions within the dynastic divisions.'

GLOSSARY

Where a pun, a metaphor or an ambiguity occurs, the meanings are distinguished as (a) and (b), or (a), (b) and (c), etc. Otherwise, alternative meanings are distinguished as (i) and (ii), or (i), (ii) and (iii). Abbreviations include the following: adj., adjective; adv., adverb; e.g., for example; etc., and so on; F1, First Folio; *fig.*, figuratively; n., noun; vb., verb.

abase: 1.2.246: (a) lower; (b) debase.

abate: blunt.

abject: servile subject.

abortive: unnatural.

abroach: set abroach: start flowing.

abroad: widespread.

adulterate: adulterous.

advantage: meet'st advantage: best opportunity.

advértisèd: informed.

affected: doth stand affected: is disposed.

after-supper: dessert.

alarum: instrumental call to arms (e.g. by drumming).

all: 4.4.226: albeit.

All Souls' Day: Nov. 2, when the Church intercedes for souls.

amendment: recovery.

and if (e.g. at 3.1.91): if.

anointed: Lord's anointed: sacramental king.

anon: very soon.

answer: (i: 1.3.194:) pay; (ii: 4.2.92:) answer for.

apace: rapidly.

apish: ape-like mimicking.

apparent: obvious.

arbitrement: adjudication.

arch (adj.): 4.3.2: extreme.

arms: 1.1.6: armour.

assurance: safety.

attainder: taint.

attend: 1.2.226: await.

attorney: by attorney: as deputy.

aught: anything.

aweless: inspiring no awe.

baited: harassed.

bar (n.): obstacle.

barbèd: armoured.

battalia: army.

battle: (usually i:) army; (ii, as at 5.3.346:) battle.

beads: prayer-beads: (hence) prayers.

bear (vb.): (i: 1.2.33:) carry; (ii: 2.2.128:) control; **bear with**: tolerate.

beaver: visor.

belike: probably.

betide: befall; **so betide**: so may it happen.

betimes: promptly.

bid: 4.4.304: endured.

blasted: 3.4.68: (a) shrivelled; (b) maimed by a curse.

blood: 2.1.93: kinship; **are let blood**: are executed.

bobbed: punched.

boding: prophesying.

boot: 4.4.65 (a) compensation; (b) makeweight; **to boot**: as well.

bootless: fruitless.

bottled: bloated.

brave (vb.): make splendid.

breathing: 1.3.60: one breath long.

Bretagne: Brittany.

brook (vb.): tolerate.

bulk: body.

bulwark: rampart.

burthen: burden.

but: 1.3.165: only.

butt (n.): big cask.

cacodemon: evil spirit.

caitiff: wretch.

calendar: almanac.

caparison (vb.): cover with trappings.

caper: 1.1.12: (a) leap in dancing; (b) perform sexually.

car: chariot.

careful : full of worry.

carnal: carnivorous.

censure (n.): 2.2.144: advice.

ceremonious: tied to formalities.

certifies: informs.

charge (n.): duty.

charm (n.): 1.3.215: (a) incantation; (b) curse.

check: rebuke.

circumstance: detailed argument.

clock: **tell the clock**: count the strokes of the clock.

close (adj.): secret, private.

closet: private chamber.

cloudy: gloomy.

cockatrice: mythical serpent that kills with a look.

cock-shut time: sunset.

cog (vb.): cheat.

cold: 1.3.312: ungrateful.

colours: 5.3.35: battle-flags.

commit: 1.1.48: arrest.

compass (n.) scope.

competitor: associate.

complaining: lamentation

complot: conspiracy.

compounded: resolved.

conceit: fancy, notion.

concluded: 1.3.14: decreed.

conduct (n.): escort.

consequence: 4.2.15: response.

considerate: critical.

consistory: council chamber.

consorted: (i) conspiring; (ii: 3.7.137:) in alliance.

consume: sap, exhaust.

conversation: 3.5.30: coitus.

conveyance with: riddance of.

cope: grapple; fight.

cordial (n.): restorative drink.

corse: corpse.

costard: large apple: *fig. for* head.

counted: acknowledged.

courage: **word of courage**: battle-cry.

cousins: 2.2.8: relatives.

cozen: cheat.

cried on: 5.3.231: urged on.

cross (n.): vexation, setback.

cross (adj.): perverse.

cross-row: alphabet.

crown (n.): (a: 3.2.43:) head; (b: 3.2.44:) royal crown.

current: valid; genuine.

curst: ill-tempered.

dally: trifle.

dance: 3.7.56: protract.

dear: e.g. at 1.4.200, 2.2.77: grievous.

deck (vb.): dress.

decline: 4.4.97: recite in order with correct endings.

deep: 4.2.116: (i) secret; (ii) perilous; (iii) full; **deep-revolving**: deeply scheming.

defend: 3.7.81: forbid.

demise (vb.): transmit.

denier: copper coin of low value.

descant (n.): variation on melody; **descant on**: elaborate on.

descry: discern.

despiteful: cruel.

device: trick.

diet: course of life.

diffused: 1.2.78: (i) contagious; (ii) misshapen.

direction: 5.3.16: judgement.

dispatch: hurry.

disposition: inclination.

dissemble: cheat, disguise; **dissembling**: cheating.

distain: defile.

Divel: Devil.

divided: 3.1.179: separate.

divine (vb.): prophesy.

dolour: grief.

doom (n. and vb.): decree.

draw in: 1.3.89: drag into.

dread (adj.): revered.

duck (vb.): bow.

duty: **do me duty**: make obeisances (bow, etc.) before me.

effect: (i: 1.2.120:) agent; (ii: 1.2.121:) result; **stand effected**: relate.

effeminate: tender.

egally: equally.

elvish-marked: deformed by elves.

embowelled: disembowelled.

empery, empire: realm.

enfranchise: liberate.

engross: fatten; **engrossed**: 3.6.2: copied larger.

entertain: employ.

entreat: 4.4.152: (a) treat; (b) address.

envious: malicious.

ere: before.

estate: (i: 2.2.127:) realm's present condition; (ii: 3.7.213:) rank.

even: 3.7.157: smooth.

excursion: armed sally, raid.

exercise: 3.2.109: (i) service; (ii) sermon.

exeunt (Latin): they go out.

exit (Latin): he or she goes out.

expedient: speedy.

expedition: 4.3.54: haste; 4.4.136: (a) haste; (b) march.

expiate: 3.3.23: completed.

eyrie: brood of eagles.

factious for: partisans for.

factor: agent.

fain: willingly.

fair (adv.): courteously.

falchion: sword.

fat (n.): 5.3.258: abundance.

fear: 1.1.137: fear for.

fearful: frightened.

fet: fetched.

figured: expressed.

Finis (Latin): The end.

flaky: flecked with light.

fleeting: fickle.

fleshed: (a) experienced; (b) bloodstained.

flourish (n.): fanfare; **vain flourish of my fortune**: (i) futile sketch of my destined state; (ii) useless embellishment of the position truly mine.

flout: taunt, gibe.

foil (n.): setting of a jewel.

fond: foolish; **fondly**: foolishly.

footcloth: (in) long ornamental covering.

foreward: vanguard.

form and model: plan.

forswear oneself: break one's promise.

forward: 3.2.46: prominent.

franked up: confined (as in a sty).

from: (a: 4.4.256:) with; (b: 4.4.259, 260, 261:) apart from.

front: 1.1.9: brow.

fulsome: 5.3.132: (a) excessive; (b) nauseating.

Furies: three vengeful deities.

gallèd: sore.

gentle: refined, noble.

ghost: **yield the ghost**: die.

giddy: mad.

gone: 4.3.20: overcome.

gossip (n.): chatterer, busybody.

go to: stop; that's enough.

grace: (i: 3.4.95:) favour; (ii: 3.4.96:) divine mercy.

gramercy: thanks.

grandam: grandmother.

gratulate: greet.

gross: stupid; **grossly**: stupidly.

grossness: coarseness.

ground: 3.7.49: underlying melody.

gull: dupe.

halberd: pole topped with an axe.

halberdier: guard bearing a halberd.

halt (vb.): limp.

hand: **set hand**: legal style.

hap: state, situation.

haply: perhaps.

happy: 3.4.6, 3.4.21: propitious.

Ha'rford West: Haverford-west: town in western Wales.

hatches: moveable planks forming a deck.

have with you: I'll accompany you.

hearse: coffin on a bier.

heavily: melancholy.

heavy: 1.3.231: (a) sad; (b) weighty; 3.1.5: sad.

helm: helmet.

hie: hasten.

hind: female deer.

hold: **in hold**: in custody.

holp: helped.

homicide: murderer.

hot: 1.3.311: eager.

Hoyday (contemptuous): Hello.

hull (vb.): 4.4.438: float with sails furled.

humour: mood.

idea: **right idea**: true image.

idle: useless.

ill-dispersing: evil-distributing.

images: 2.2.50: sons.

imaginations: **unfelt imaginations**: 1.4.80: rewards imagined but not experienced.

impeachment: accusation.

incapable: uncomprehending.

incense (vb.): incite.

index: prologue.

indirect: devious, deceitful.

induction: preparation; prologue.

inestimable: 1.4.27: (a) invaluable; (b) countless.

infection: pestilence.

infer: (i: 3.5.73:) allege; (ii: 3.7.12 , 4.4.343:) cite; (iii: 3.7.32, 5.3.314:) state.

instalment: installing.

instance: 3.2.25: basis.

intelligence: information; **intelligencer**: spy, agent.

intend: (i: 3.5.8:) suggest; (ii: 3.5.8, 3.7.45:) pretend.

intestine: internal.

inward: intimate.

issue: children.

iwis: certainly.

Jack: vile low-born man.

jealous: jealous (stretched in F1 to aid metre).

jet: 2.4.51: (a) encroach; (b) strut.

Jove: Jupiter, ruler of the Roman gods.

jump (vb.): tally.

keeps: 5.3.29: stays with.

kind: (i: 1.4.231:) naturally loving; (ii: 3.7.211:) affectionate.

kite: scavenging bird.

labour: 1.4.236: work for.

Lady: **by'r Lady**: by the Virgin Mary.

lag: late.

lap (vb.): wrap.

late: 3.1.99: recently.

leads (n.): roof-edge.

leisure: (i: 5.3.97: a) limited leisure; (b) pressure; (ii: 5.3.101:) ample time.

Lethe: underworld river of oblivion.

level (vb.): aim.

lewd: base, low.

lie for you: 1.1.115 (a) take your place; (b) tell lies for you.

liege: lord.

light (adj.): 3.1.118: (a) trivial; (b) light in weight.

lightly: readily.

like (vb.): 3.4.49: please.

limit: appoint.

livelihood: lively animation.

Lord's anointed: king, deemed divinely chosen, anointed with 'holy' oil.

lour: glower, scowl.

luxury: lechery.

main: 1.4.20: ocean.

malapert: impudent.

malmsey-butt: big cask for sweet wine.

manners: (i: 3.7.191:) polite customs; (ii: 4.4.207:) morals.

mark (vb.): listen to.

marry: 1.3.98–100: (i) by St Mary; (ii) wed.

mean (n.): 1.3.90: cause; **open means**: unimpeded access.

measure (n.): dance.

meed: reward.

mercy: **cry . . . mercy**: (I) beg . . . pardon.

Mercury: winged messenger of the Roman gods.

mere: outright, sheer.

methought: it seemed to me.

mewed; mewed up: confined, caged.

milksop: spoilt weakling.

miscarry: 1.3.16, 5.1.5: die.

misconster: misconstrue.

misdoubt: worry about, fear.

moe: more.

moiety: half.

monuments: 1.1.6: trophies.

moody: angry.

mortal: 5.3.124: living; **mortal-staring**: 5.3.90: (i) causing death by staring; (ii) staring at death.

movables: personal property.

murther: murder; **murtherer**: murderer.

muse (vb.): wonder.

naught: mischief.

noble: gold coin.

nice: 3.7.175: trifling.

nods: **French nods**: elaborate bowing.

nomination: naming the day.

nonage: minority, youth.

nought: nothing.

novice: youth.

object (vb.): 2.4.17: apply.

obsequiously: mournfully.

occasion: **on what occasion**: for what reason.

o'ercloyed: excessively full.

o'erlook: 3.5.16: (i) look out over; (ii) inspect.

o'er-worn: worn-out.

office: function.

one: **all's one for that**: it doesn't matter.

open (adj.): 4.2.75: unimpeded.

opposite: 4.4.216: hostile.

orient: lustrous.

out: **will out**: will become known.

overblown: ended.

overgo: surpass.

overweening: arrogant.

owe: own.

pack-horse: work-horse.

pageant: play.

painted: 1.3.241:
(a) counterfeit;
(b) adorned by cosmetics.

palpable: obvious.

parcelled: piecemeal.

parlous: 2.4.35: (a) perilously shrewd; (b) mischievous.

part (n.): **take in gentle part**: kindly approve.

part (vb.): divide.

party: 1.3.138, 3.2.47, 4.4.191: side.

passing: surpassingly.

passionate: 1.4.112: compassionate.

pattern: example.

Paul's: St Paul's Cathedral.

pawned: pledged.

peevish: perverse.

peise: weigh.

pell-mell: headlong.

Pembroke: town in western Wales.

perfit: perfect.

perforce: necessarily; forcibly.

period: 1.3.238: conclusion.

Pilate: Pontius Pilate, who washed his hands of Christ's death-sentence.

pilled: pillaged.

piping-time: time for pastoral pipe-playing.

pitch (n.): 3.7.188: apex.

politic: shrewd.

Pomfret: Pontefract Castle in Yorkshire.

post (vb.): hasten;
in all post: at great speed.

post-horse: speedy horse;
packed with post-horse: sent speedily.

prate: prattle.

precedent: 3.6.7: original.

prefer: promote;
preferment: promotion..

presently: at once.

prime of: early.

prithee: **I prithee**: I beg you; please.

process: (a) story; (b) course.

prodigious: monstrous.

prolonged: postponed.

proof: strongest armour.

proper: handsome; 3.7.125: own true.

Protector: guardian of, and ruler for, a young king.

prove: test.

puissance: power.

puissant: powerful.

pursuivant: messenger authorised to serve warrants;

pursuivant-at-arms: military messenger.

quest: 1.4.174: jury.
quick: (i: a: 1.2.65:) alive; (i: b: 1.3.5, 3.1.155:) lively; (ii: 4.4.361:) hasty.
quicken: enliven.
quit: (a) requite; repay; (b) pay for.

rags: 5.3.328: beggars.
rankle: 1.3.291: cause a festering wound.
razed off: torn off.
reason: 2.3.39: converse.
recomforture: consolation.
Recorder: chief legal official for London.
recure: cure.
reduce: lead back.
reft: bereft.
remembered: been remembered: recollected.
remorse: pity.
repair: return.
replenished: complete.
report: 4.4.153: noise.
resolve: answer.
restrain: 5.3.322: seize.
retreat . . . sounded: trumpets call for a withdrawal of troops.
revenue: income.
Rood: Cross.
royalty: 3.4.40: sovereignty.
rude: 2.2.38: blatant.
rue: regret.
runagate: renegade, turncoat.

Saint George: patron saint of England.
scathe: harm.
score (n.): 1.2.256: twenty.
scrivener: scribe and copyist.
seasoned: garnished.
seat: 1.3.112: throne; **seated:** 2.4.60: (a) enthroned; (b) settled.
sennet: musical flourish at an entry or departure.
sequel: sequence.
servant: 1.2.206: (a) menial; (b) lover.
servitor: leaden servitor: slow servant.
set hand: legal style.
several: separate.
sharp-provided: resourceful.
shouldered: 3.7.128: (i) shoulder-deep; (ii) shoved.
shrewd: sharp.
shrift: confession.
sign: 4.4.90: mere symbol.
sirrah (addressing an inferior): my man.
sit about: 3.1.173: meet to discuss.
sleepy: 3.7.123: dreamy.
slug: idler.
sluggard: tardy sluggard: late-waking idler.
soft (interjection): wait; be calm.
something: somewhat.
sop: small wine-soaked cake (or bit of bread).
sort (n.): gang.
sort (vb.): find.

speed (vb.): succeed, prosper.

spent: **day is spent**: well under way.

spleen: (i: 2.4.64:) malice; (ii: 5.3.350:) wrath.

splinted: bound in splints.

spoil (n.): 4.4.290: (a) prey; (b) slaughter.

springing: spritely.

spurn: trample.

stall (vb.): install.

stand: **stands me much upon**: is important to me.

state (n.): 1.3.112: rank.

staves: 5.3.341: lances.

stay (n.): support.

stay (vb.): stop.

still: constantly.

stop (vb.): 5.5.40: (i) staunch; (ii) cease.

stout: bold.

straitly: strictly.

stripling: youth.

strook: advanced.

struck in years: advanced in age.

suborn: induce.

suddenly: speedily.

suffer: allow.

suggestion: 3.2.100: instigation.

suit (n.): entreaty.

surfeit: excess.

suspects: suspicions.

sweets: fragrant flowers.

swelling: inflated by wrath and pride.

swill (vb.): guzzle.

tall: brave, manly.

tane: taken, captured.

teen: grief.

temper (vb.): steer.

tender (vb.): cherish; **tend'ring**: cherishing.

tender (adj.): young.

tetchy: fretful.

timeless: untimely.

timorous: fearful.

title: 2.2.48: legal right.

toy (n.): trivial item.

tract: course.

tractable: compliant.

train (n.): entourage.

trick: **sportive tricks**: (a) amorous bouts; (b) frolics.

troth: faith.

unblown: unopened.

unavoided: unavoidable.

unfashionable: badly shaped.

unhappiness: wretched state.

unknown: 1.2.217: secret.

unlooked: unforeseen.

unmeritable: unworthy.

unrespective: unobservant.

unvalued: priceless.

urge: (i: 1.3.146:) cite; (ii: 2.2.137:) provoke.

usurp: (4.4.109: a:) wrongly take; (4.4.110: b:) encroach on.

vail: yield.

vantage: advantageous aspects.

vassal: wretch.

vaunts (vb.): flaunts his power.

ve'ment: vehement.

verge: **inclusive verge**: enclosing rim.

visor: mask.

vouchsafe: consent.

wait upon: attend.

want (vb.): (i: 3.7.125:) lack; (ii: 2.1.43:) need; (iii: 3.1.6: a) lack; (b) desire.

wanton: randy.

ward (vb.): guard.

warn: 1.3.39: summon.

warrant (vb.): assure: **in warrant**: authorised.

wash (n.): hog-wash, pig-swill.

watch (n.): 5.3.63: (i) watch-candle, night-light; (ii) sentinel.

wayward: erratic.

welkin: sky.

well-spoken: eloquent.

whe'er: whether.

wherefore: why.

whet: urge.

while: **breathing while**: time for a breath.

white-livered: cowardly.

widow-dolour: grief of widowhood.

windows: 5.3.116: (*fig.*:) eyelids.

wingèd: flanked.

withal: (i: 1.1.103:) nevertheless; (ii: 1.3.133:) in addition; (iii: 3.7.57:) with; (iv: 4.4.278:) with it.

witty: astute.

wonderful: extraordinary.

worry (vb.): 4.4.50: rip.

wot: know, knows.

wrack: (i: 1.2.127:) destruction; (ii: 1.4.24:) wreck.

wracked with: destroyed by.

wrong-incensèd: (a) mistakenly provoked; (b) aroused by wrongs.

yeoman: farmer or freeholder below rank of gentleman.

Zounds: By God's wounds.

THE WORDSWORTH CLASSICS'
SHAKESPEARE SERIES,

EDITED BY CEDRIC WATTS:

BOOKS BY CEDRIC WATTS:

Conrad's 'Heart of Darkness' A Critical and Contextual Discussion.
Milan: Mursia, 1977; 2nd edition: Amsterdam: Rodopi, 2012.

Cunninghame Graham: A Critical Biography (with Laurence Davies).
Cambridge University Press, 1979; paperback edition, 2008.

A Preface to Conrad. London and New York: Longman, 1982;
2nd edition: London and New York: Longman, 1993.

R. B. Cunninghame Graham. Boston, Mass.: G. K. Hall,
Twayne, 1983.

The Deceptive Text: An Introduction to Covert Plots. Brighton:
Harvester; New York: Barnes and Noble; 1984.

A Preface to Keats. London and New York: Longman, 1985.

William Shakespeare: 'Measure for Measure'. Harmondsworth:
Penguin, 1986.

'Hamlet'. Brighton: Harvester; New York: Barnes and Noble;
1988.

Joseph Conrad: A Literary Life: London: Macmillan; New York:
St Martin's Press; 1989.

Joseph Conrad: *'Nostromo'.* London: Penguin, 1990.

Literature and Money: Financial Myth and Literary Truth. Hemel
Hempstead: Harvester, 1990.

'Romeo and Juliet'. Hemel Hempstead: Harvester Wheatsheaf;
Boston, Mass.: Twayne; 1991.

Thomas Hardy: 'Jude the Obscure'. London: Penguin, 1992.

Joseph Conrad. Plymouth: Northcote House for the British
Council, 1994.

A Preface to Greene. London and New York: Longman, 1997;
digital edition: Harlow: Pearson Education, 2003.

Henry V, War Criminal? and Other Shakespeare Puzzles (with John
Sutherland). Oxford: Oxford University Press, 2000.

Thomas Hardy: 'Tess of the d'Urbervilles'. Tirril: Humanities-Ebooks, 2007.

Joseph Conrad: 'The Secret Agent'. Tirril: Humanities-Ebooks, 2007.

The Connell Guide to Thomas Hardy's 'Tess of the d'Urbervilles' (with Jolyon Connell). Chippenham: Connell Guides, 2012.

Final Exam: A Novel (by 'Peter Green'). London: PublishNation, 2013.

Fantastic Finds of Ann and Ron: Stories in Verse for Bright Youngsters. London: PublishNation, 2014.

The Connell Guide to Shakespeare's Second Tetralogy. London: Connell Guides, 2014.

Shakespeare Puzzles. London: PublishNation, 2014.